Praise from:

HEALTH CARE PROFESSIONALS:

This book is a beautiful example of parent insight, dedication, and understanding. Trudy's description of her personal experience with tragedy and suffering, gives a unique opportunity for parents and professionals of various fields to further their understanding of depression. My hearty endorsement and gratitude for this book. *Jerome Kwako M.D., Fellow American Academy of pediatrics; Director, ADHD Clinic, Miller Dwan Hospital; Director, Comprehensive Clinic for Children with Handicaps*

"Well written and thoughtful. An interesting personal account of the symptoms of depression and anxiety. Carlson has done a very nice job of covering a difficult subject." *Dr. Carrie Borchardt, Division of Child and Adolescent Psychiatry, School of Medicine, University of Minnesota*

PARENTS:

"Insightful, educational yet easy to understand. Interesting and comforting. The purpose of this book is to reduce the unnecessary pain of depression for the individual as well as for their family and friends who also feel the effect of this condition -- a most profound goal. " *Monica Natzel, mother of a 15 year old suicide victim*

"In sharing your very personal and painful story with the rest of us, you enlighten the general public regarding the many dimensions of the tragedy of depression which, unfortunately, is increasing among young people today. " *Rosanne Biever, mother of four*

TEACHERS:

"Trudy Carlson's account of Ben's struggle with depression is a very helpful book. Even before its publication, I have recommended it to the parents and teachers I know who are struggling with similar problems in their families and classrooms. " *Jo Stewart M.S., English Teacher and Speech Coach*

"An open-hearted, detailed account of one mother's struggle. I was struck by the enormous effort it takes to care for someone with an illness such as Ben's Trudy writes with precision and clarity. Her willingness to dig deep : soul will heal others who are looking for comfort and guidan~ *Blatnik, M.A.E.S., English and Composition Instr~*

Publisher's Note

The information in this book regarding illness is intended to raise the awareness of the symptoms of depression, attention deficit hyperactive disorder, and anxiety disorder in young people, as well as the potentially effective treatments for these conditions. It is not a substitute for the advice and directions of your personal physician. It is not meant to encourage anyone to take any medications or make changes in the way current medications are taken without first consulting your doctor.

THE LIFE OF A BIPOLAR CHILD
What Every Parent and Professional Needs to Know

By Trudy Carlson

Benline Press, Duluth Minnesota

Benline Press, 118 N 60th Avenue East
Duluth, Minnesota 55804

Publisher's Cataloging in Publication Data
Includes bibliographical references and Index
1. Depression in children
2. Depression in children - treatment
3. Attention-deficit-disorder children
4. Manic-depressive illness in children
5. Child psychology
6. Children – suicidal behavior

TABLE OF CONTENTS

PART I THE STORY

PART TWO: THE FACTS BEHIND THE STORY

ACKNOWLEDGMENT

No book is the product of just one person. My heartfelt gratitude goes to everyone who contributed to it. I want to thank those individuals who read this work in manuscript form at various stages. They include: Roseann Biever, Caroline Carlson, Lu Harter, Char Gallian, Margaret Kinetz, Monica Natzel, Carol Nord, Rod Nord, Jo Stewart, Nancy Scheftner, Dr. Elisabeth Kubler-Ross, Dr. Barry Garfinkel, Dr. Kenneth Irons, Dr. Jerome Kwako, and Dr. Carrie Borchardt.

I would like to make special mention of Kristen Oberg, Patt Jackson and Robin Blatnik, the editors of the book, whose skill and encouragement helped to make it what it is. Their sustained commitment to this project is the kind of help writers dream of receiving, but never expect to get.

I wish to express appreciation to all the works that are quoted in this book. The list of these are contained in the bibliography.

There can be no full accounting of the debt I owe to the scores of people who contributed to this project by giving me advice and/or technical assistance. They include:
Dr. Aaron Beck, Martha Hellander, Joseph Gallian, Sheldon T. Aubut, Ann Sanford, Melanie Horn, and Marj Cox.
Special thanks to my brothers and sisters and close friends who helped in a number of ways.

The cover is designed by David Garon.

Preface

Much of this book first appeared in 1995 in my book The Suicide of My Son. After its printing, I was approached by some individuals, whose interest was to help the general public learn more about depression in young people, to divide that book into smaller, comprehensive halves. Consequently, Part 1 is now published as Ben's Story: The Depression, ADHD, and Anxiety Disorder That Caused His Suicide. Part 2 is now Depression in the Young: What We Can Do to Help Them.

In 1998 a parent of a bipolar child mentioned that my book was the first published account of a child with manic-depressive illness. She requested that I reprint my original book in a slightly modified form for the benefit of parents and professionals who want to know more about this condition. She lamented the fact that all too often this condition goes undiagnosed and untreated because too few people understand it.

It is my hope that is revised, updated and expanded book will help the children who suffer the pain of this illness, the parents and teachers who need to find the means to help them learn to cope with it, and will help medical professionals more readily diagnose and treat this condition.

Introduction

I t isn't surprising that before World War II few pediatricians or psychiatrists would not have diagnosed bipolar (manic-depressive) illness in children. What is heartbreaking is to realize how few children in the last decades, when the incidence of this condition has risen, are still not being diagnosed and treated.

Although there are many theories about why the incidence of unipolar and bipolar depression has risen since then, no one can say for certain why this is. The dramatic changes we experience during this century which brought about the reduction of established traditions and the guideposts which gave structure and stability to our lives may be a contributing factor. Parents of children suffering from unipolar or bipolar illness may feel that these youngsters have, in a sense, been cursed by a condition that is the results of factors outside of anyone's control.

I thought I was alone in my frustration at not being taken seriously when I reported that the symptoms my son exhibited were identical to my husband's symptoms. It seemed fairly obvious to me that both were suffering from an illness with a strong genetic predisposition and that the diagnosis of bipolar illness applied to both of them. I assumed it was because I was "just Ben's mother" that my observations were discredited.

When I attended the Second International Conference on Bipolar Illness in Pittsburgh in 1997, I was saddened to hear that eminent child psychiatrists and researchers such as Dr. Joseph Biederman of Harvard University, Dr. Barbara

Geller of Washington University, and Dr. Elizabeth Weller of the University of Pennsylvania were sometimes as frustrated as I was in their attempt to bring forth their findings on bipolar children. They report that when they sent the results of their studies to scientific journals, these findings were sometimes seriously questioned because "there wasn't mention of this condition in the literature." But how can there be mention of this condition in the literature when studies of these children are rejected?

Why attempt to break the vicious cycle of ignoring this significant health problem? First and foremost is the pain it causes the child. If a child breaks his leg, or has a headache, we don't ignore it. Yet few people understand just how painful bipolar illness can be. When we think of depression, we often envision a sad or crying person. But anger and irritability is just as likely to be manifested as sadness. The angry child hurts. Bipolar children often report headaches, tummy aches, and pain in their arms and legs. The pain of this condition manifests in many ways.

Second is the pain it causes the family. What parent doesn't hurt when their child is hurting? What brother or sister of a child with bipolar illness isn't affected by the disruptive behavior of an ill sibling?

Third is the problem it creates in school. Teachers try their best to work with these children. Most youngsters with bipolar illness have more symptoms of attention deficit hyperactivity disorder than children who have ADHD. The inability to concentrate, the hyperactivity and impulsivity, the hallmarks of ADHD, are especially prevalent in the vast majority of children with bipolar illness making these youngsters difficult to work with *if* they are not being successfully treated with medications and therapies.

Fourth is the likelihood that the illness may cause more disability if it goes untreated. We need to think of all forms of depression like we do any other illness. Although the human body is a miraculous thing capable of healing itself, we would never think of not putting a broken leg in a cast simply because our bodies will naturally mend at the site of the break. Physicians apply a cast to insure that as the bone heals naturally, the bone will be straight with no permanent disability. Children with bipolar illness suffer assaults from incidents of depression and mania or hypomania. Undiagnosed and untreated, many scientists hypothesize that these repeated incidents create disability when the brain of the growing youngster learns to become a victim of the illness.

Fifth is the financial cost of failure to treat. We all know that the cost of hospitalization can be ruinous. Even if your family does have to pay the cost of hospitalizing someone with bipolar illness, most of us pay insurance. Wouldn't those premiums be lower if the general public was healthier and not in need of expensive care? When it comes down to dollar and cents, the cost of effective outpatient care for both bipolar and unipolar depression is significantly less than the cost incurred when these conditions go untreated.

Finally, there is the hidden but very real cost to society as a whole. This includes the reduced ability to prepare these youngsters to become productive members of society; the reduced productivity as workers for those young people who do manage to find and stay in jobs; and the potential antisocial behaviors for those unfortunate victims of this condition who experience problems with anger and aggression. Truly bipolar illness is not only a serious social and health concern, but one that we simply cannot afford to ignore. But bipolar illness is not always easy to understand, in fact some of it is baffling.

My son Ben's illness came to him at an earlier age and was more serious than my husband's as a child. This was a mystery to me. My husband's childhood, was marked by the chaos of financial instability, frequent changes in residences and schools, that would be expected when one's father's manic depressive illness was undiagnosed and untreated. Because the emotional storms my husband experienced from his father contributed to the pain of his childhood, Garry was determined to spare his children from that kind of suffering. Consequently, he was diligent about seeking and cooperating with medical treatment.

There was no financial instability in our marriage. Luckily, I am blessed with good health and Garry and I both try to meet the challenges of life with humor rather than anger. When Ben showed signs of being even more seriously ill and more disabled at a younger age than Garry at the same age, it didn't seem to make sense.

I now know that this has a scientific name: *anticipation.* The combination of the cohort effect (the rise of incidents of all forms of depression since WWII) and anticipation (the tendency of a few genetically based illnesses to become more serious and onset at an earlier age in succeeding generations--in bipolar illness this might occur when they are passed from the father's line of the family) makes depression in general and bipolar illness in particular an important conditions for all of us to learn about.

Ben's Bipolar II illness is probably even less recognized than children with Bipolar I. Children with Bipolar I illness have manic behaviors that are so disruptive and intrusive that few parents and teachers would miss the fact that there is something seriously wrong with the child.

Children with Bipolar II illness have hypo (little) mania. Less troublesome, it is more likely to be missed. However, the pain of the depression experienced by people with Bipolar II illness is among the most painful of all the depressive conditions. Furthermore, although Bipolar II patients are not hospitalized as often as those with Bipolar I, they often experience more disability. Thus, failure to diagnosis and treat this condition in youngsters is nothing short of tragic.

This book is one attempt to reduce the ongoing tragedy. The good news is that there is a virtual explosion in what is being learned about the brain. Man has been on the planet for millions of years, but most of the scientists who are learning so much about the genetics and functions of the brain are alive *right now*. Drug companies are developing and testing medications that are proving to bring about mood stability. Anticonvulsants as well as lithium are proving to be extremely useful medicine for bipolar illness. New antidepressants with fewer side effects are being tested and brought on to the market all the time. Psychological interventions with proven effectiveness such as cognitive / behavior therapy and interpersonal therapy can and have made a great deal of difference in the lives of those who suffer from these conditions. They are as essential a part of treatment for most depression as is education about the illness and proper diet is for the diabetic.

The news about the discovery in the science of the brain and the advancements made in treatment is excellent. The big hurdle facing child and adolescent psychiatry is one of educating parents, teachers, psychologists, guidance counselors, doctors and psychiatrists about the symptoms of bipolar illness in children. It is my hope that this book will help.

Infancy

How did Ben's life start?   When I think about the beginning of his life, it is enlightening to compare Ben's birth and infancy to that of our first child, Caroline.   The birth of our daughter was a wonderful experience.   I was thrilled about the pregnancy, and since she arrived the day before my own birthday, I felt she was the best present any woman could ever receive.   I will never forget my reaction to her birth. My response to her was surprise: surprised that somehow this bulge in my body turned out to be a baby.

At the time, I was a twenty-seven year old instructor at the university teaching child development classes.   I knew perfectly well this bulge was a baby, but there was nothing logical about my feelings of surprise.   My reaction was an emotional one based on my being taken aback by the magic and wonder of life itself.

My second reaction came a day or two later, when Garry and I fell head-over-heels in love with this little creature. We both commented how it felt as if we were fourteen years old again and had fallen in love for the first time.   Her birth had the feeling of springtime, when the world is fresh and new.   Our experience of loving this child was so special to us that we were convinced no other parents had ever loved a baby as much as we loved our beautiful daughter. This is total nonsense, but who ever said anyone in love is sensible?

The year was 1971 and doctors kept mothers in the hospital for five days. This delivery left me feeling physically exhausted.   During the first four days of my hospital stay, I was glad to be taken care of and happy to have someone else tend my baby. By the fifth day, I was rested and ready to go home. When I took Caroline home she was on a regular four-hour schedule: she would sleep for three hours, and then there was the one hour in which to change her diaper, feed her four ounces of formula, burp her, and put her back to bed. She had this four hour cycle which included the infamous 2 a.m. feeding for about six weeks. After that she began sleeping through the night.

How different things were with the birth of Ben. I was just as happy about my second pregnancy as I had been about my first. I had wanted to become pregnant again when Caroline was eighteen months old, but because my husband was going through a career change and finances were a little uncertain, I had delayed getting pregnant for an additional year. Ben was very much the long-awaited, welcomed addition to our family. When I told Caroline that she was going to have a sister or a brother, I asked her what she would like to name the baby. She answered, "Betsy." We had many delightful talks about the new Betsy coming to live at our house.

I was due on Thursday, March 13. I felt that I had started labor on two separate occasions earlier that week, but it had stopped each time. On my due date I had an appointment with my doctor, and told him what had happened. I requested to be admitted to the hospital on the weekend so labor could be induced. He told me that he usually preferred to let nature take its course, but if I insisted, he would proceed with the induction. It seemed to me that the baby and I were ready, so I made admittance plans for Friday.

When I entered the hospital Friday evening, the atmosphere in the maternity ward was tense. It seemed every woman there was having some sort of complication. The first woman I saw was in labor prematurely. If it was determined that they could not stop the labor, chances were the baby would need to go to the infant intensive care unit. The next person I saw was a student in one of my classes. His wife was in labor with twins. The following day she had two daughters, one of whom had spina bifida. These newborns were taken very quickly from the delivery room to the intensive care unit.

My own process of being induced started all right, but was temporarily interrupted because several hospital personnel were needed to handle the care of the twins. The staff got back to me as soon as they could, and continued the medication that would induce labor. After a time, my doctor decided to break my water since that would assist the process. It was then he discovered Ben was coming shoulder first rather than head first. (Perhaps this was the reason the labor, which started twice earlier in that week, had stopped each time.) My physician told me he would have had to do something to assist the birth. The doctor repositioned Ben by pushing back on his shoulder, thus allowing him to came head first. The birth occurred very quickly after this.

When the doctor said "It's a boy!" I was surprised. After so many months of calling him Betsy, it took me a few minutes to get used to the idea. Also, since I spent the preceding three and a-half years with the identity of "a mother of a daughter," it was going to take me some time to get used to the change. I remember thinking, with amusement, "Not only is he a boy, but he is ugly." I do not know if it had anything to do with the days of waiting to be born or simply from the process of birth itself, but initially Ben did not look that great. Surprisingly, within five minutes, Ben's face sort of re-arranged itself and he turned into an exact replica of the baby I had had three and a half years earlier.

Later a nurse would take the receiving blanket off Ben's little body to show me he was perfect, with all ten fingers and all ten toes. A healthy beautiful boy: how lucky we were to have him! But my attention did not seem to be focused on my new son. I felt depressed and found myself crying in my room. Dr. Gold, an expert on mood disorders, tells us that "The vast majority of women (70 to 80 percent) endure `maternity blues.' Frequently, on the third day following delivery the new mother becomes tearful, sleepless, tense , and angry. Episodes come and go for twenty four hours to a week, then they lift" (Gold, p. 281). In my case, I was not unwilling to relate to my baby nor was I unhappy about his arrival. What I felt was overwhelming sadness about the fate of the babies born that day and sorrow for the mothers who bore them. I especially focused on the baby with spina bifida. I knew the parents, and because I had some experience with this condition, I was sorry for what they might go through in the future.

As I wept in my hospital bed, I cried for this new little baby girl with spina bifida, knowing it was possible this child would have the pain of growing up feeling different, sometimes excluded. Being different, even in cases where the differences do not seem great, can create a major gulf between a child and its peers. Sometimes the peer group may not even detect any difference, but if the child feels different, he will feel not quite at home in the world. In my hospital room I thought I was crying for this new little girl, for her pain, and the pain her parents would feel in the upcoming years as they saw her excluded from some of the simple joys of life.

How paradoxical life can be! Looking back on it now I see that although I was thinking about this little girl, what I really was seeing was a preview of my own son's life. It would be my son whose inability to concentrate would make it difficult to comprehend the strategies and rules of games like baseball and football. It would be my son who would feel "different". The "manic quantities of physical and emotional energy" associated with his bipolar (manic-depressive) illness would make it difficult for him to get along with or play easily with other children. His attention deficit hyperactive disorder (ADHD) and his anxiety disorder would also be a factor in these problems. His multiple problems would cause him to exclude himself or be excluded from many activities. It would be my heart that would break as I saw him being excluded. My efforts to find some way to help him fit into the mainstream would be frustrated.

The little girl born on that day died in a year. My son coped for as long as he could with a dysfunction created by a genetic condition. People with bipolar illness inherit a predisposition to the illness. Scientists are now trying to pinpoint the exact genetic marker for this disorder. Little by little, I would come to understand what it is to care for an infant with depressive illness.

On Ben's first full day home, I began to see that he did not have an easy schedule. He did not want to drink all of his formula, and he was not able to sleep for consistently long stretches of time. Eager to leave the hospital and get back home to my husband and daughter, I left the hospital sooner than I would have had to go. By the second day at home, I concluded I may have made a mistake rushing to get back. When I had stayed in the hospital five days with my daughter, I took home a baby who had an easy four-hour schedule. The nurses, I concluded, must know how to manage these newborns in a way that produced this pattern. Rushing Ben home early had not allowed the nurses time to produce the wonderful scheduling of three hours sleep and one hour feeding.

This would prove to be the first of many times I would conclude that Ben's difficult behavior was the result of something I had done, or failed to do. He was having problems eating and sleeping: two of the classical markers of depression. He showed these signs at four days old!

I hope I will not be misunderstood here. I am not saying that every baby who has trouble with eating and sleeping is going to grow up with bipolar illness. What I am saying is that my child had a genetic condition which affected him throughout his life, and it was marked enough for me to remember a warning sign which showed up at four days old. Also, the problems of people with bipolar illness are not a result of environment or rearing. Research indicates that children with bipolar illness generally have good mothering (Gold, 1987).

As the weeks went on, I tried to deal with Ben's eating and sleeping problems in a number of different ways. If I could get Ben to drink larger quantities of formula at a time, I thought he would sleep for longer periods. No matter what I did though, he would drink about two ounces of formula and fall asleep. I would jiggle the bottle back and forth to try to get him to suck, but it did not work. He would sleep for an hour or so and wake up hungry.

This frequent need to be fed occurred around the clock. Instead of a single 2 a.m. feeding, Ben required several nighttime feedings. Furthermore, this behavior did not stop after a month or two. As he got older he would drink more than just two ounces but continued to waken during the night throughout his babyhood. When he was six, seven, and eight months old I was still usually getting up once or twice during the night to give him a bottle.

Dr. Popper has observed that this is a common occurrence for infants with bipolar illness. In his article Diagnosing Bipolar Vs ADHD, /(Attention deficit, hyperactive disorder) he writes: "During infancy, certain bipolar children do not sleep through the night to establish an overnight sleep pattern until 8 - 12 months, or even until four years of age." I do not remember how old Ben was when he finally slept through the night. My guess is he was still waking once during the night past his first birthday. I would just hand him a bottle and stagger back to bed hoping to get more sleep. This continuous feeding had a negative effect on his new baby teeth, causing him dental problems later on.

I did all sorts of other things to help him sleep through the night. I tried a strategy that had worked when my daughter was an infant. When she was old enough to start eating cereal, I would give it to her late in the evening just before I wanted to go to bed myself. When I tried things like this with Ben, they did not work to help him sleep through the night. I even tried giving him a bath in the evening, knowing baths usually tire babies out, but nothing worked. The standard "just let him cry without feeding him" did not work, either. When I called my doctor in desperation for some help in getting this seven month old infant to sleep during the night, he suggested that I try putting a little decongestant into his bedtime bottle for a few evenings. He thought after a few nights a longer sleep pattern would develop. The decongestant did improve the condition, but no pattern developed. Without the decongestant, Ben did not sleep through the night.

By telling the story of Ben's life, I hope to illustrate that depression in children is the same as depression in adults, but the symptoms are slightly different. For example, depressed adults have sleep disturbances. Infants with depression may not sleep through the night. Depressed adults either do not eat enough or eat too much. Infants with depression are frequently underweight, or like Ben, have other eating problems. Depressed adults may have problems with constipation. Ben's difficulties with constipation began as an infant and continued throughout his childhood. Depressed adults can experience aches and pains in their bodies. As an infant, Ben usually cried each day for about an hour or so. Nothing I could do -- no amount of rocking him or walking with him -- succeeded in comforting him. I have often wondered about the source of his discomfort. I can not be sure it was caused by the depression, but it is certainly a possibility in view of the aches and pains he reported later in childhood. ADHD children also may show signs of agitation as babies, so not all of Ben's fussiness in infancy may have been caused exclusively by his bipolar illness, but the eating and sleeping problems probably were.

Preschool

Much of this chapter describes Ben's impulsive, dangerous behaviors. Children with attention deficit hyperactive disorder are predominately characterized by impulsivity which sometimes results in posing a danger to themselves. Describing what life was like for Ben in his preschool years helps to make the connection between these dangerous behaviors during those early years and his impulsive, self-destructive act of May 31, 1989.

Ben started to walk at twelve months and was a very active youngster from that point on. The terrible two's started for Ben at eighteen months, when he began climbing out of his crib. Ben was determined to get out of his crib and did not seem to care if he got hurt in the process. I decided it was better to lower the side of the crib and let him climb out safely rather than risk injury.

Our children were sharing a room in the two bedroom house we lived in at the time. Now that Ben was no longer confined to his crib, our five year old daughter, Caroline, was not able to play without Ben disrupting her activities. An inability to play quietly and cooperatively with others is typical of toddlers, but Ben was particularly difficult. To reduce friction between the children, we purchased bunk beds. Caroline could then play on the top bunk if she wished to get away from Ben's interference. We bought the beds, set them up and felt everyone had a way to relax.   My relaxing was to come to an end exactly one week later. I was resting on the bottom bunk and keeping Ben company while he played in the room. Caroline was on the top bunk. I had my eyes closed and was enjoying the relative peace and quiet when I heard Caroline say, "Good Ben, you climbed up here". My eyes shot open. My eighteen month old had climbed up the back of the bunk bed and was now on the top. I grabbed him and put him on the floor, but once again he climbed up the back of the bunk bed. That night my husband and I lifted the top bunk off and the children ended up with two single beds.

So, at eighteen months, Ben was in a regular bed and not confined in any way. This would not have been a problem if it were not for his tendency to engage in dangerous behaviors. For example, Ben often put things into electric outlets. We bought plastic plugs to put into the receptacles. Ben would just remove the plugs and proceed to put things into the outlets. He received shocks a number of times; I once saw sparks come out of a socket. Ben cried, obviously in pain, but he continued to poke his finger and other things into the light sockets. It was not as if we did not tell him "no" and move him away from the wall, but Ben was a very determined little boy.

Another of his favored play areas was the stove. From his age of one-and a-half to three-and-a-half, I never used the oven because Ben wanted to open the door and crawl in. I needed to be sure the oven was not only off, but cool. Recently, my daughter told me a story about little Ben which dramatizes my need for caution regarding the oven.

One night when we were out, the baby-sitter became terrified because she could not find Ben. She and Caroline ran around the house looking for him. The sitter went down to the basement twice looking for Ben. The second time she came back up and walked through the kitchen she heard a knock coming from the oven. Looking through the glass on the door she saw

Ben's little face smiling at her. She screamed! Apparently Ben had discovered that after he climbed into the oven it was possible for him to hit the door with his hand in such a way that the door would close behind him. Can you imagine what would have happened if she have decided to heat the oven to make a pizza?

Ben also loved the burners on top of the stove. Twice he took pans of boiling water off the burner. We were always careful to put pans on the back burners with the handles pointed in, but Ben would then grab the side of the pan. The first time he did this he received a small burn on his arm. It formed a blister about the size of a quarter. The second time he did not get burned at all. The boiling water went all over the floor but it missed Ben completely. Once when he was small, I ran down to the basement to quickly put a load of clothes in the washer. I returned to find him sitting on a burner playing with the knobs. Luckily, again, he was not burned.

Finding ways to safely confine Ben for the times we could not watch him took much effort and time. We hit on the idea of cutting off the top part of his bedroom door, making it into a Dutch door. His room then would become something of a large play pen. At eighteen months, Ben could climb out of a regular sized play pen, but until he mastered the art of turning knobs, he would be safe playing in his room. He could look out over the top of the door and not feel shut in. We could check up on him and know that he was all right.

A year later we moved to a new three bedroom house. The property on which we built our house had a log cabin playhouse in the backyard. During the next year I furnished the playhouse with a 9 x 12 foot rug, a small bed, a combination oven and sink, and an old chair. I put an old shelving unit in one corner and added lots of discarded dishes. Some of them were little plastic plates and bowls, but I also had some glassware. I had thought of just throwing away those mismatched glasses, but standing with them in my arms poised over the garbage can, I thought about the playhouse and decided my daughter would enjoy playing with them. I had furnished the playhouse with my seven year old daughter and her girl friends in mind. I was not thinking about little boys.

One afternoon, when four year old Ben was playing a little too quietly with the three year old neighbor boy, I thought I should investigate. When I opened the door to the playhouse, Ben was standing with a croquet mallet poised high above his head, about to smash a glass. The rug was totally covered with broken glass. The neighbor boy was watching.

My thought was, "If either of those boys fell, they would be cut from head to toe!" I told them both to freeze. First I grabbed the neighbor boy and took him out of the playhouse. Then I grabbed Ben and took him out. I told the neighbor to go home and Ben to go to his room. I then cleaned up all the broken glass, removed the few remaining unbroken glasses, and put them all in the garbage. I knew I had to impress upon Ben the dangerous nature of what he had done. What was I to do to help him understand? I can not remember all that I did, but it included a long, serious talk.

Some parts of Ben's preschool years had not been that different from Caroline's. Both my children had been very active with a general lack of interest in quiet activities such as coloring or putting puzzles together, but there were definitely differences between them. Caroline tried to include Ben in her games and he tried to fit into them, but there were always problems. She had been in several family daycare settings as a young child where she played with a number of children. Caroline also played in her neighborhood "gang." She says Ben was the type of kid one could not play with. She described how Ben would get to a certain point where he would just lose control. He would become overly excited, or overly aggressive, or overly sensitive, or tearful. In one way or another, he would be disruptive of their play. After a time, Caroline and her friends concluded that it was just easier to exclude him, and they avoided playing with him.

A neighbor of ours has said nearly the same thing. Ben would often go to her house to play. Her children would play with him for a time, but the outcome of their games would always be the same: Ben would end up feeling hurt and would return home in tears. Ben had an overly-sensitive nature and an enlarged reaction to everything. He was an active child, but it was not wild hyperactivity in which the child is constantly in motion and disruptive. It was more like an intensive reaction to specific situations. When he was having a good time, he would become too exuberant and silly. When he was angry, he would get furious. Ben cried easily and often. Sometimes when his crying was especially long and hard, he would vomit.

During the period between age two-and-a-half and three-and-a-half, Ben did not seem to develop many new skills. I remember thinking "he was a year older and a year bigger, but developmentally he was about the same as he was a year earlier." Ben also had a peculiar speech habit: whenever he would say anything, he would mouth the last few words of the sentence silently a second time. (Other signs of speech/sentence structure peculiarities would show up later.) I now know that both slowness in processing information and speech can be a sign of depression.

As Ben got older and was involved in nursery school and kindergarten, he continued to display dangerous behaviors. He had three injuries during the 18 month period starting from February 1980 to August 1981, the periods from when he was not quite five years old until just past his sixth birthday.

At dinner one evening we were finishing our meal and discussing what was for dessert. Ben knew we had some ice cream in the freezer unit on the top portion of our refrigerator. Impatient for the rest of us to finish our meal before dessert was served, Ben climbed to the top of the counter to get a dish for the ice cream. Perched there, he was also in a position to open the freezer unit. Suddenly he lost his balance and tumbled to the floor. He was crying as I picked him up, and he said his head hurt. I comforted him as much as I could, but he was in a lot of pain.

The next morning his head was fine, but when I dressed him he winced as I put on his shirt. He pointed to a place on his shoulder that hurt. I sent him to the sitter as usual. At dinner he still reported pain in his shoulder. Later that night I was with some friends, and I told them what had happened. I made light of the situation, as the latest of many experiences with this boy who was continually getting into trouble. My friends were concerned about the pain in Ben's shoulder, and they suggested I take Ben to the doctor. The next day Ben cheerfully gave the doctor an account of his adventure climbing the counter to get himself some peppermint bon-bon ice cream. It was obvious to me how charmed both the doctor and his nurse were by this spunky little boy who enjoyed talking with adults.

An x-ray confirmed what my doctor suspected, a broken collar bone. My reaction was "Oh my God, he's had a broken bone for almost two whole days, and I have ignored it by not getting treatment for it." I felt terrible about this. My doctor immediately became surprisingly firm with me, telling me to stop all this guilt business. It was uncalled for and not appropriate in this case. He reassured me that a slight delay in getting treatment is no reason for feeling guilty, and would have no negative affects. I was taken aback by the strength of the statement in this generally mild-mannered, cheerful man. I was also deeply grateful to him. Ben wore the little shoulder brace for six weeks, and the shoulder healed just fine.

About six months later, Caroline got a new two wheel bike for her birthday. Ben wanted to try riding it and Caroline let him. I sat on the front steps outside my home watching all of this. I told Ben he was too young to ride the bike, but if he promised to stay on the large blacktop area in front of the garage or ride it on the lawn he could ride if for a short time with supervision.

It was such a pleasure to watch them. It did my heart good to see Caroline willing to share her new bike with her little brother, especially since Ben had difficulty playing with other children. Ben was thrilled, and I was thoroughly enjoying myself when the phone rang and I went inside the house to answer it. Caroline and her playmate also needed to go into the house at that time. Ben saw his chance to take the bike out onto the sidewalk. Our neighborhood is on a slight incline. If Ben rode down the sidewalk he would be able to go pretty fast. This would be a lot more exciting than just going around and around in circles on the blacktop as I had asked him to do. The fact that the blacktop or grass would make a softer landing than concrete for a child learning to ride a bike apparently was not an issue with Ben.

I was talking on the phone when I suddenly heard an ear piercing cry. It would be years before I would actually find out all the details of what happened, but Caroline tells me that the front wheel of the bike hit a lead pipe on the land between the sidewalk and the street. When Ben fell off the bike, his head hit the sidewalk. The girls heard Ben crying and ran out to see what had happened. They brought him into the house with a very sore head.

The next morning Ben was still reporting some pain, so I called the doctor. I told him that as Ben cried about the pain, he would become very upset and vomit. The doctor wanted to know if Ben often vomited when he cried hard. As I mentioned earlier, many typical day-to-day events would set Ben off emotionally into crying long and hard, which sometimes did cause him to vomit. The doctor felt Ben probably had a concussion from the fall, but there was not much we could do. Ben's head would hurt for a week or so, and we would see some vomiting during that time. Rest and time was the only treatment for the injury.

About a day later, the top and back of his head began to feel soft, and I panicked. What if Ben did not simply have a concussion? My fear was that he might have some other, more serious, injury. I did not know what was wrong, but I suspected the worst when I felt his soft head. I again called my doctor.

The softness was probably caused by blood collecting between the skull and the scalp. The doctor said Ben's body would naturally absorb it over time, and we would just need to wait for the process to occur on its own. In a kindly, nonjudgmental way, he indicated that since ice was not applied at the time the injury occurred, there really was not anything we could do now except wait for it to go away.

As the days went by, I kept feeling the back of Ben's head. It seemed to be getting softer. This was also Garry's impression. I was trying not to panic or be upset, but that is easier said than done. During the weekend I had lots of time to observe Ben's head and lots of time to worry. At the end of two days of non-stop fear, I took Ben to the emergency room to have them check it. Just going through the process of once again talking about the injury with medical personnel seemed to relieve the pressure of my concern. They reassured me that there was not anything abnormal about the swelling, and since it was not a new injury there was not anything they could really do to help me. Nor could they give me any answers to my concern that Ben's head seemed to have gotten a bit softer in the last couple of days. They were sympathetic and told me it would likely take a few more days before we would begin to see absorption of the blood. They were very polite, but a little confused as to why I was bringing an old injury to the emergency room. My answer to this was that there are probably few things that are quite as unnerving as to have the back of your child's head feel like a marshmallow. To our relief, a few days later the swelling did go away.

The following June, Ben had his third accident. He had just finished kindergarten and it was the first day of summer vacation. I was out of town at an all day meeting. I got home around 6 p.m., but there was no one around and this made me a little nervous. The doors were open, the windows were open, and there was no note on the kitchen table explaining everyone's whereabouts. The place had the feel about it as if people had left hurriedly or unexpectedly. I brushed this impression off and thought Garry had decided to take the children out for hamburgers and fries. We usually eat at five and they would have been back by six. Rather than worry, I decided to try to enjoy the peace and quiet. I went into our bedroom to make the bed when the phone rang. It was Garry.

He started with some pleasantries: "Hi, how are you? How was your drive?" I gave him brief answers, all the time thinking "What is going on?" Then Garry said, "I am here at the emergency room at the hospital. Ben has a broken arm and they are taking him to surgery." I rushed to the hospital fearing that Ben might have some permanent damage to his arm.

It was not long until we were able to speak to the orthopedic specialist. Ben had broken both bones in his arm, at a point several inches above the wrist. The procedure they did is called a closed reduction because they did not have to open the skin at all to set the bones. Setting the two bones without anesthesia would have been an extremely painful process, and no one would have expected Ben to be able to lie quietly while the doctor did it. I was glad the emergency room doctor had called in a bone specialist to work on this bad break. He cast it from the wrist up over the elbow. The specialist told us it would probably take at least eight weeks to heal, but there would be no permanent damage. This was a relief! (See the picture of Ben with the cast on his arm seated with our favorite baby sitter, the one who had the oven scare.)

The accident occurred in a neighbor's yard, while Ben and his friend were playing on a ladder. Ben's playmate had climbed off the ladder and had gone into the house. Ben decided to do an experiment with the ladder -- attempting to use it as a pair of stilts! Despite what we have seen in old comedy movies, ladders do not make very good stilts. When the ladder fell, Ben's forearm was probably caught on the wrong side of a rung as it hit the ground.

That night I stayed in the hospital, sleeping when I could, on a couch in a waiting room just outside Ben's room. Several times during the night he woke up crying. I would go into the room, rub his forehead and cheeks until he fell back to sleep. The next morning a policeman came into Ben's room. He was very cheerful and pleasant. I thought "Isn't it wonderful of this off-duty officer to come to visit the children's unit of the hospital? Young children idealize anyone in uniform; What a thoughtful thing to do." It only occurred to me later that this was no off-duty officer, but someone performing an investigation! After all, this was Ben's third serious injury in an eighteen month period. One would not expect a child to have that many "accidents" in such a brief period of time.

The police officer did not stay in the room long. I was totally naive about why he was there and left the room shortly afterwards to go downstairs for breakfast. The officer went back into the room to question Ben after I had left. Many years later, when Ben and I were talking about his broken arm, he told me the officer wanted to know how things were at home: were we good to him, did we fight a lot, etc.

I am not offended in the least by the investigation. At the time, I had not known it occurred and when I found out I thought it was amusing. I asked Ben what his reaction was, as a six year old, to talking with the officer. He said, "I knew what he was doing. I was not about to tell him anything about our family."

After Ben's death, as I was talking with his therapist, she reminded me about those high-risk behaviors Ben had as a boy.

She said the fact he made it to fourteen was, in many respects, a tribute of the care we had given him. This helped me to put things a bit in perspective. Another thing that helped to give some perspective was to compare Ben's history of injuries with that of my childhood family. I grew up on a farm with seven siblings. Because of the machinery and large animals, farms can be very dangerous places. To hear that a farmer lost an arm or even his life in an accident is not uncommon. Yet all eight of us children managed to work on the farm and never break a single bone. If you multiply eight children by a minimum of 18 years you get a total of 1,728 months without a broken bone. Compare this with Ben. Here was a boy who had two broken bones and a concussion within eighteen months!

Ben's preschool years were difficult for me, but there was one aspect that was a real godsend. While I worked each day, Ben was cared for by a fantastic elderly couple, Mr. and Mrs. Backstrom. (Ben called them Grandma and Ray. See his picture with them) Their attachment to him was symbolized by the nickname they gave him: "Peanuts Backstrom." I could not have asked for a better child care situation for this overly sensitive, yet warm and loving child. Their house was as much a home to him as was ours. They had more time and patience to give to him than I did. They would play games with him, set up their camper in the back yard as a playhouse for him, and generally treat him like a cherished grandchild. Ben, in turn, adored them. No child was more fortunate in his day care than Ben.

With all the loving attention Ben was getting at the Backstrom's house, I did not feel motivated to send him to preschool. But as kindergarten approached, I decided to send him to a nursery school for part of the year to help him with the transition. There was a program three mornings a week not far from our home.

Ben was a little hesitant in his interaction with the kids at nursery school, but I did not see anything particularly unusual. At the end of the school year, the teacher met with the parents for a conference. She told us Ben was neither strong nor weak in any area. He was a typical kid and ready to start kindergarten next fall. But it was Ben who made an astute observation about himself.

There was a little four-year-old girl who came to "Grandma's" a few mornings a week. She was able to do a lot of things Ben was not able to do. For example, she was beginning to learn how to read, and it was coming easily and naturally for her. Ben wondered how it was possible for a child one year younger than himself to do things that he could not do. His life experience thus far had taught him that the older you were, the more you could do. Since this little girl was younger, her more grownup reading skills did not make sense to him. It was the first of many experiences in which other children were able to do things he could not do.

The summer after nursery school, Ben began having a problem with bedwetting. Toilet training had gone fairly well for him; at 24 months he had insisted on using the toilet. Grandma Backstrom called me to report how Ben had cried that day, insisting on using the toilet. She said he acted as if he knew what the toilet was for and suggested we give toilet training a try. Ben did use the toilet, but he also frequently wet his pants. We discontinued the training after a few weeks, thinking we should wait until Ben was a little more mature.

In August, when he was two-and-a-half, I tried again to toilet train Ben using praise and rewards, but got the same results: he willingly used the toilet, but wet his pants often. Since this method had not worked, another option was to use a different approach. I told the summer baby sitter that we would probably have to punish Ben for wetting. This is the opposite of what I had used to train Caroline. Praise and reward for using the toilet were effective for her, but with Ben the reverse seemed necessary. Rather than needing to learn when to use the toilet, he needed to learn when not to wet. This discipline actually worked very quickly for Ben, whereas praise and reward had been getting us nowhere. I recall Caroline telling me she thought the sitter was mean when she had Ben stand in the corner for wetting, but Ben was both day and night trained with this system within a week.

Early in June, when Ben was five years old, he suddenly started wetting the bed each night. Ben had wet the bed occasionally during the three years since being trained, but never like this. I assumed he had a bladder infection, but the urine sample I took into the doctor's office was negative. Ben drank a lot and urinated often, so my second guess was diabetes. The doctor's tests for that were also negative. Our physician suggested a one month trial of imipramine an anti-depressant with a side effect of urine retention.

The month-long trial of the imipramine did not significantly reduce his wetting, and we were then referred to a urologist. The doctor examined Ben and scheduled him for a kidney x-ray. The general findings were negative. Surgery could have been tried, but we were told it had only limited probability of solving the problem. Concerned about the possible terrifying effect surgery might have on a small boy, and the low probability of helping the wetting, we felt it did not seem worth the risk.

Ben continued to have some bedwetting throughout childhood, which probably hurt his self-esteem. None of our efforts improved the situation: decreasing liquids before bedtime, trial elimination of specific foods from his diet to test for allergies, waking him in the middle of the night to go to the bathroom, commercial devices to awaken him when he wet, or behavior modification. Finally, we simply put a plastic cover on his mattress, and got used to doing a lot of laundry. We also tried not to make a fuss about the wet sheets in the morning when they occurred.

It may seem paradoxical that this little boy, who later would be diagnosed as having depressive conditions, did not respond with complete success to antidepressants when given them at age six for bedwetting. Unfortunately, depressed children do not always do well with tricyclics such as imipramine. Also, the level prescribed for bedwetting is not a therapeutic dosage for depression. So although he had a problem with depression and was being treated with an antidepressant, the medication at that dosage was unfortunately ineffective for either the bedwetting or the depressive mood.

Bedwetting is another symptom associated with depression and anxiety in children. I now feel strongly that Ben's first major depressive episode may be dated as beginning on June 5, 1980, when his nightly bedwetting started. Although Ben was chronically depressed, I feel his first major mood swing may have occurred that June.

Early School Years

W hich of Ben's school problems were caused by his depression, which were related to his anxiety disorder, and which were due to his attention deficit hyperactive disorder? Separating them out is a big order, because some of the symptoms overlap. Here I will emphasize the symptoms that may be more related to his depression during his early elementary years, but ADHD will of necessity be included.

Ben's first year in school went all right. His teacher felt the kindergarten year should be exclusively devoted to social adjustment. She wanted children to be comfortable about coming to school. There was little pressure to perform, which made his kindergarten year a pleasant one for both Ben and me. At the end of the year, I went to the conference with the teacher. She explained that although she could not put her finger on it, she felt Ben might have some difficulty with school. How right she was!

INABILITY TO CONCENTRATE, SPEECH PECULIARITIES

In first grade, Ben had an excellent teacher who felt that reading was what first grade was all about. Unfortunately, Ben was turning out to be a weak reader. His biggest problems in school were his difficulty attending to tasks and getting his work done. His teacher began sending home his unfinished work and I began what became an ongoing process of making sure Ben completed his assignments.

At the end of first grade, his teacher and I agreed the best thing for him was to forget about school for the summer and concentrate on the things he wanted to do, such as swim and ride his bike with us. Garry and I felt this was especially important since his broken arm the previous summer had made those activities impossible. We decided to hope for the best, and perhaps by next fall he would be a little more mature.

Ben continued to have difficulty paying attention and completing assignments in second grade. At conference time in November, we discussed his problems with Ben's teacher. She thought Ben's problems were medical, and suggested he see a physician.

I took Ben to a pediatrician who had experience with children who had learning problems. The doctor recommended a three-day evaluation at a comprehensive clinic but suggested we wait until Ben was in third grade. The doctor found that the diagnostic team could be more accurate when the child was nine years old rather than only seven or eight. He could schedule Ben for the evaluation the next year.

I had observed something wrong with the way Ben talked. His articulation was fine, but his sentence structure was faulty. When he spoke, some of the words of the sentence were out of order. I requested a speech evaluation be done at Ben's school. The therapist met with me first to discuss my concerns. During our conversation, I mentioned our plans for the three day evaluations at a comprehensive clinic during third grade. The speech therapist shared her experience with medical evaluation of children with school problems. Often the finding is that there is nothing medically wrong with the child. Some parents are relieved to hear this, while others are upset that money had been spent on the evaluation and the child's school problem continues without any help toward a solution. She suggested we consider requesting an evaluation by the learning disabilities (LD) teacher there at the school. This would be done at no cost to us. Her suggestion made a lot of sense.

The results of the speech evaluation showed that Ben's speech was all right, and his vocabulary was within normal limits. I realize now that what I observed in Ben's speech is part of what psychiatrist Dr. Charles Popper described as "cognitive looseness."

COGNITIVE LOOSENESS

According to Dr. Popper, children with either attention deficit hyperactive disorder or bipolar illness have speech that is hard for the listener to follow. These children "can give disorganized narratives and make logical leaps that are non-psychotic but still hard to follow." For example, when Ben described what happened in a TV program, the story he told was not in consecutive order. It would be extremely difficult for the listener to figure out what actually happened on the TV program.

This "cognitive looseness" would naturally cause problems in reading comprehension. When a child can not even clearly describe what happens in a story he has both heard and seen on TV, it is easy to understand the difficulty he would have in making sense of a story he had read. Further, if the child does not comprehend what he is reading, there is little logic or pleasure in reading at all. Such kids, obviously, are not motivated to read. Depressed kids are often described as unmotivated. Little wonder!

During third grade Ben continued to struggle with his work and I continued to help him with it. One of the assignments each week was for him to write a story. The teacher would help the children get the story started by giving them the first three or four sentences. (Coincidentally, I had used this same technique when I taught elementary school and found it enormously successful.) Since Ben had difficulty functioning on his own, he often brought home this assignment with very little completed. We would re-read the beginning sentences and discuss various possibilities of how to finish the story. In these assignments, I again saw examples of the "cognitive looseness," -- disorganized narrative which made "logical leaps that are not psychotic but still hard to follow." In Ben's writing, I saw the written form of this cognitive looseness. His narratives were jumbled; they did not make sense.

OPPOSITIONAL BEHAVIOR

The diagnostic category "oppositional" behaviors is controversial among child and adolescent therapists. It describes a youngster who, as the term implies, does not do what parents, teachers, and other adults ask him or her to do. Some mental health professionals question whether there really is a disorder such as this, or if the child's unwillingness to comply is a natural outgrowth of being asked to do things that are difficult. No one who knew Ben would have said he was abrasively defiant, but anyone who tried long and hard to help him get his daily work done would have experienced a form of this problem.

The official diagnosis of oppositional behaviors have gone through an evolution during the last years. According to the DSM -IV oppositional defiant disorder occurs when :

A. A pattern of negativistic, hostile, and defiant behavior lasting at least 6 months, during which four (or more) of the following are present:

1. often losing temper;
2. often arguing with adults;
3. often actively defies or refuses to comply with adults'
      requests;
4. often deliberately annoying people;
5. often blaming others for his or her mistakes or misbehavior
6. often being touchy or easily annoyed by others;
7. often being angry and resentful;
8. often being spiteful or vindictive;

B.   The disturbance in behavior causes clinically significant impairment in social, academic, or occupational functioning.

Like every problem Ben had, the symptoms showed themselves gradually.   During the summer following second grade, rather than send him to summer school to catch up, I had him do some very short review math sheets at home. Ben's reaction was to complain often and try to negotiate a reduction of the assignment.   Ben wanted both to achieve and to be excused from doing the work it required.   Often during his elementary years, when things would not go well for him, Ben would tell me we were not strict enough. It was as if he did not have enough internal structure or discipline to control himself, so he wanted something from the outer world to impose restrictions and control over him. He knew the other kids were able to handle school and other life situations. He saw that the parents of his friends expected a lot from their children and were firm. He wanted to succeed and wanted us to be strict enough to produce this result. The paradox is that when I would attempt to organize his time by giving him constructive activities, he would spend a great amount of energy trying to get out of doing them.

Sometimes the structures I would set up would be developed by both of us sitting down and negotiating a plan. One example of this was the amount of TV he could watch; the number of hours spent on school work would equal the number of hours in which he was allowed to watch TV. Plans like that worked out fairly well for him. Ben, like many depressed kids, could spend excessive amounts of time watching TV rather than engaging in social or sports activities. Setting some limits to TV watching by making it contingent on the child's activity was helpful.

As Ben got older, I would sometimes tell him about all the work I had to do when I was his age. Ben would say, "Mother, you're you. You can do that stuff. I'm me. I'm different." And of course he was right. If Ben had not had an attention deficit disorder and a depressive illness, he would have been able to do what I wanted him to do, what his teachers wanted him to do, and what he probably wanted to do. But when something is wrong with a child, some of these goals may not be possible.

ILLNESSES DURING EARLY ELEMENTARY SCHOOL

Ben's childhood was plagued with frequent illnesses. I am not sure how much of this illness can be attributed to depression and how much of it might have been allergies, but I know Ben had many more colds, flu, stomach aches, headaches, and ear infections than most kids. If there was anything to catch during the school year, Ben caught it. My husband and I wrestled over whether to make Ben go to school when he was not feeling well or to keep him home. If he stayed home every time he was not feeling well, he would miss a great deal of school. We did not want him to have even more problems because of absences; he would also have a lot of makeup work to complete when he finally did return. Further, since Ben did not seem to like school, we feared he would use sickness as a way out.

Often when we sent him to school he would feel fine, but other times he would feel miserable all day long. Occasionally, the teacher noticed Ben's inattentiveness, and sent him to the nurse's office. We finally discovered a solution which allowed him to stay home but did not reinforce being sick; it also encouraged him to make good use of his time. He was not to watch TV, and he had to be in bed where he could sleep, read, draw, or use his educational toys. I called his teacher in the morning and asked her to send home Ben's assignments. I would either pick them up myself or a neighborhood boy would bring them to our house. Ben did the assignment that afternoon and evening so was not behind in his work.

I do not think Ben's illnesses were fabricated. His temperature was real, the cough and congestion were real, the pain in his head or ears was real, and the vomit was real. I can not be certain whether the cause of his physical illness was his depression (because depression does affect one's immune system), if Ben had allergies which may have caused some of these symptoms, or if the illnesses were caused by a combination of depression and possible allergies. I only know the situation was uncomfortable for everyone.

After lots of problems with colds and congestion, Ben developed a hearing problem. An ear specialist recommended tubes be put in; this necessitated day surgery.

ATTEMPT TO GET A DIAGNOSIS / MISUNDERSTOOD BY OTHERS

When fourth grade began, I continued to help Ben every evening with his homework. Ben was making a lot of errors when he did his assignments. I wanted him to have some success with his work and to learn to work carefully. To help him with this problem, I would check his assignments after he had done them, and erase all the incorrect answers. I would have him re-do those items that were wrong.

I worked with Ben to produce correct assignments for two reasons. First, since doing schoolwork was so torturous for him, I did not want him to go through the process of actually finishing the work only to receive an F because of the errors. I wanted him to have some chance of getting reinforcement and have a reason to keep trying. If his errors were found and corrected, his odds of doing acceptable work would improve. Second, I wanted to reinforce the value of doing the work carefully and correctly the first time. The fewer errors he made, the fewer he would have to re-do.

But this process of identifying errors and correcting them made Ben angry. He felt he had gotten the work done and now I was insisting that he re-do part of it. I do not know if this was part of an oppositional defiant disorder or just a typical reaction.

I thought Ben had a learning problem, and I wanted him to get services in the school so he could do some work there. As fourth grade began, I went ahead with the request for an evaluation by the learning disabilities (L.D.) teacher.

Ben's aptitude (what he is capable of doing) was compared to his achievement (what his actual performance was) in those subjects. His aptitude was approximately one year higher than his achievement in both reading and math. The findings of the evaluation meant he did not meet the eligibility requirement for services as learning disabled. With no help from school forthcoming, I looked into the possibility of getting someone else to help him with homework. I contacted a former elementary teacher and asked him to work with Ben each day after school. Arrangements were made for Ben to catch the city bus after school and go to his tutor's home for approximately two hours of help. He would then catch a bus home. Ben went to this tutor for several months and later, when the teacher was unable to continue doing the work, I hired an older student to take over the tutoring for the last few months of the year.

ANGER AND IRRITABILITY

During the spring of Ben's fourth grade year I became influenced by the work of Elisabeth Kubler-Ross. She is most well-known for her work on death and dying, but I heard her give a talk at a conference for persons interested in children with learning problems. She spoke on the importance of communicating to children that your love for them is not based on their behavior or their work performance. Specifically, she advised parents to hug their children at least once every day and tell them they are special, a gift from God; you will always love them no matter what.

Children's television personality, Mr. Rogers, conveys much the same message. He often says things like: "I like having you in my neighborhood because you are special," "I like you because you are you," and "I like you just the way you are." When my children were younger and watched his show, I often wondered whether Mr. Rogers made this statement at the close of each program because it was the one thing he wanted them to remember most of all.

After hearing Dr. Kubler-Ross's powerful lecture, it was clear to me that I had been right to change my focus to giving Ben reassurance rather than help with his homework. I decided to concentrate on giving him unconditional love while he received help with his homework from someone else. I am glad I took this approach. For about two years I made sure I hugged Ben at least two or three times a day and told him he was special, a gift from God, and I would always love him no matter what. After a time I found he seemed less angry. Shortly before he died, Ben told me that of all the things we did to help with his depression, the one thing that seemed to work best were the hugs and statements of unconditional love. This is why I feel so strongly that emotional support is essential in any program for students.

I remember a Mother's Day card he wrote. It told me he would always love me no matter what. Right now the memory of this card is very precious to me.

Upper Elementary Years

FIFTH GRADE

W hen Ben entered fifth grade, he had two teachers: a morning teacher and an afternoon one. Ben liked both of his teachers very much and his promotion to upper elementary school was uplifting to him. He wanted to perform well for these teachers, but his difficulty getting his work done, legibly and on time, continued.

My husband, Garry, decided this would be the year he would volunteer to take over the nightly homework supervision. The first half of the school year seemed to go well, but during the second semester I would often hear Ben crying in his room late at night. One night when I went in to comfort him; he said that he wanted so much to do well in school, but he always seemed to do poorly. He wanted so much to get A's and B's on his own, but no matter what he did or how hard he tried, unless he got help he always got D's or F's.

In the past, when we had attended parent/teacher conferences, Ben's difficulties were often described as problems with work habits and motivation. As I sat there listening to Ben I thought, "Do children with motivational problems cry in their beds at night because they aren't doing well in school?" It did not make sense to me. I told Ben I knew he sincerely wanted to do well, and I was going to find a way to help him. Ben's response was, "You have no idea what it means to me to have someone who understands."

I went to the next scheduled meeting of an association of parents who have children with learning disabilities. One of their pamphlets described some of the symptoms which included:

1. short attention span (restless, easily distracted)
2. reverses letters and numbers
3. personal disorganization (can not follow simple schedules)
4. impulsive and inappropriate behavior (poor judgment in social situations, talks and acts before thinking)
5. inconsistent performance (can not remember today what was learned yesterday)
6. speech problems (immature speech development, has trouble expressing ideas)

All of this sounded like Ben to me!

At the parent's meeting, I found out there was going to be a conference the following month on learning disabilities. I decided to attend. I also decided to find out what other resources were available in our city for children with learning problems. I contacted the Human Development Center to find out if they had any suggestions regarding tutors. A therapist told me that the Language Therapy Center in our town evaluated children and then referred them to a tutor who is trained in the Orton Gillingham method, a system used for young people with dyslexia (reading, spelling, and writing problems).

My attempts to get someone to recognize the true nature of Ben's problem led me to attend the conference on learning disabilities in April of 1986. It was there I learned that dyslexia is a problem of brain anatomy, while attention deficit disorder may be more a problem with brain chemistry as it relates to the functioning of specific parts of the brain. I also learned that some young people with learning disabilities commit suicide, especially when depression occurs along with the learning disability. The speaker mentioned that a small dose of antidepressant medication is often helpful to patients with ADHD.

Later the same month, I scheduled Ben for an appointment at the Language Therapy Center in our city. In the therapist's opinion, Ben had a mild form of dyslexia. Specialized tutoring was recommended. The minimum length of the program was two years with the student meeting with the therapist three hours per week for one-hour sessions. A trained tutor lived fairly close to our home, and Ben began lessons soon afterwards.

Some of the evaluator's observations of Ben were insightful. She wrote:

Ben was cooperative and friendly during the entire period. He took the initiative, beginning and completing all requested tasks promptly. He was verbally facile. His conversation was at a much more mature level than his written work. He seemed much older than 11 years old. He was quick and accurate on lots of the testing. When things became difficult on the spelling and writing tasks, his errors became more evident. He tried to please, however.

Looking back on her comments, I find them to be an accurate description of Ben when his depression was not particularly acute. Her comment on his maturity was especially important. Most adults, when meeting Ben for the first time, got the impression Ben was precocious, not disabled. I often wonder if this was not part of the reason Ben never was able to get the academic help he needed; he did not seem to need it.

At the conference at the end of fifth grade, I met with both teachers to share my conviction that Ben had a learning problem, not just a motivation problem. One of these men had spent some time as a teacher of exceptionally bright children. Now as a teacher of a regular fifth grade students, he challenged his students by giving them at least one discussion question each class period designed to really make them think. He would stretch the minds of the average students while giving the bright students a challenge. His comment about Ben was intriguing. He said, "If that boy could ever get his act together about doing his work, he could really go places. Quite often he gives the most astute, insightful answers of any student in the class." To me, this again pointed to Ben's maturity as well as the potential buried under the combination of attention deficit, depression, and anxiety disorder.

At this conference, I mentioned that Ben was evaluated and would likely receive services from the Language Therapy Center. I also requested a re-evaluation for learning disability services from the school system. Ben was again evaluated by the LD teacher in May of 1986. At the end of the month, we met with the LD teacher, the school psychologist, one of his fifth-grade teachers, a sixth grade teacher he would have the following September, and the principal. Her findings from individualized testing were essentially the same as they had been early in fourth grade: Ben did not qualify for services.

The whole process of attempting to obtain help for my child was very painful. Most other students did twice as well as my son did with less effort. The unfairness of the situation was discouraging for all of us. I understand why many young people give up trying.

In my frustration that spring, I went through the lecture notes I had taken during the learning disabilities' conference. Once again I was impressed by the work quality of the neurologist, Dr. Drake Dune, from the Mayo Clinic in Rochester, Minnesota. It occurred to me to take Ben to the Mayo Clinic for an evaluation. The clinic was only a five hour drive from our home. The question still remained in my mind: was Ben's problem a matter of work habits and motivation, or did he, in fact, have a learning disability? If we could not get a definitive answer to the question at the Mayo Clinic, I felt we probably could not get an answer any place else either.

When I had comforted Ben as he cried that night about his problems with school, I told him I felt his problems were not his fault, but resulted from some sort of learning problem. I told him I was determined to find out what it was and to get him the necessary help. A few days after our conversation, Ben emerged from his bedroom where he was attempting to do his school work, and said to me, "Maybe my problem is that I am just plain lazy." I smiled at him and thought, "How many adults have the psychological honesty to take a good hard look at themselves and conclude that some of their problem is of their own making?" My respect for my son grew that day. It is true that Ben was not the most ambitious child, but this is also true of many other children who do just fine in school. It is hard to know what role the depression had in Ben's inability to stay concentrated or to do his work, and what role the attention deficit played. The inability to concentrate is a classic symptom of both conditions.

Ben was given an appointment at Mayo for the following September, several months away. In the meantime, I wondered if we could start the small dosage of the antidepressant mentioned in the lecture by the Mayo neurologist as being helpful to some children with attention deficit. The medication sometimes helps with the sleep disturbance and thus improves alertness the next day. Ben had reported having a great deal of trouble getting to sleep and feeling tired the next day at school. I hoped the medication would help him.

I took Ben to a local psychiatrist in hopes he would see the benefits of starting him on an antidepressant medication. The psychiatrist noted in his report that Ben had been referred because of problems with insomnia. Ben told him he was sick often and had frequent headaches. The psychiatrist noted that Ben had unreasonable feelings of guilt about many aspects of his life. Ben shared with the doctor his pervasive fear of "being goaded into some kind of excessive action" when with peers. This last symptom may reflect Ben's impulsivity, another common symptom of both attention deficit and bipolar illness. The psychiatrist decided not to prescribe the antidepressant, recommending instead we wait for the Mayo evaluation in September.

Summer came and Ben started the specialized tutoring. Besides this, I thought about the suggestion made during the conference on learning disabilities -- to accentuate skills and talents the individual possessed rather than concentrating only on areas in which the child had difficulty. Since Ben had a strong interest in computers and seemed to have some talent in that area, I registered Ben in a keyboarding class at summer school. We purchased a computer that summer, and Ben began to work with it.

SIXTH GRADE

In September, Ben had his appointment at the Mayo Clinic. It was a three day evaluation and covered everything: blood work, hearing and vision testing, an electrocardiogram and an electroencephalogram, speech and educational testing, appointments with a psychologist and a psychiatrist, and an interview with the neurologist -- the expert of learning disability I heard lecture in spring. Ben enjoyed his adventure at Mayo. He thought of Mayo as the Disney World of Medicine. He liked their high-tech, yet friendly, approach.

During the appointment with the neurologist, Ben spoke alone with him for about thirty minutes; then I was called in to join them. The doctor felt Ben did not have dyslexia because his reading in this one-on-one setting was not that far below grade level. Ben's performance in reading seemed more characterized by a hesitancy or unwillingness to do it, rather than an inability to read. He also wondered why Ben was so mature. Ben was 11 1/2 at the time, and the neurologist said that Ben's manner and conversation was more mature than he usually sees from 14 or 15 year olds. (This had been the same impression the other evaluator had of Ben.)

At the end of the three days, I attended the summary conference where the results of all the testing were presented. The team recommendations were made at this time. There were three significant observations: First, Ben's verbal IQ was at the 77th percentile, while his performance IQ was at the 37th percentile. This meant verbally he was above average, but he performed below average. Second, Ben had a noticeable emotional dysfunction. Third, he had a mild but significant difficulty with attention.

They recommended Ben begin an antidepressant medication for the attention deficit; he should be considered for LD services at school in the areas of spelling and written language; and he should see a psychiatrist on an outpatient basis for at least a trial period. When presented with these recommendations, Ben was vehement about not wanting to see a psychiatrist. He felt seeing a psychiatrist would label him as different and defective. Also, he had been upset by his experience with a psychiatrist the previous spring and did not wish to see this doctor again.

I assured Ben that no one was going to push him into something against his will. At that time, our community did not include a psychiatrist who specialized in adolescents. Going to a larger city for appointments would require a six or seven hour round trip each time. I would have to do some research about whom he should see, and that would take time.

When the November teacher's conferences were set up, we wrote a note to his teachers letting them know we would share the Mayo report with them. At the meeting, we met with one of his teachers who showed interest in the report. His other teacher did not attend the conference and later called us complaining that Ben was doing some of his school work on the computer rather than writing it out by hand. She felt allowing him to turn in typewritten work would be treating him differently from the other children, a practice of which she did not approve.

The next month we had a meeting with the principal and both of Ben's teachers. This is the first conference in which I felt the system was listening <u>to</u> us rather than talking <u>at</u> us. I mentioned the importance of Ben seeing some hope and not despairing. There had been several suicides at our local high school that year, and I mentioned what the neurologist had said about young people with learning disabilities and depression being at risk. At this conference the school agreed to accept some of his homework done on the computer. It was also decided not to grade Ben at all on handwriting. The remaining time in sixth grade seemed to go fairly smoothly. Ben was receiving private tutoring in reading skills, Garry was helping him study for tests at school, and I was continuing to provide emotional support.

Seventh Grade

H ow would Ben cope with junior high? He was always a totally disorganized child. How was he going to cope with 6 different classrooms and 6 different teachers? Ben's elementary teachers might have been frustrated in their attempt to work with him, but they at least became accustomed to his problems. They were with him all day and came to realize that Ben was basically a nice boy for whom school was a struggle. Would his junior high teachers just view him as a non-compliant student?

Then there were the challenges from peers. Ben was overly sensitive and lacked social skills; thus he felt uncomfortable with other young people. How was he going to cope with so many unfamiliar fellow students? Additionally, it is typical for 9th graders to harass the incoming 7th graders. What would the hazing process be like for him during this first year? Peer pressure becomes a major issue as students enter the teen years. Since Ben had very limited impulse control, he was especially vulnerable to being led into problem behaviors. What kind of trouble was this thirteen, fourteen, and fifteen year old going to get into in junior high?

When a young person has problems learning in school, the gap between what he can do and what other students his age can do widens each year. Would this cause him to view himself as neither one of the "good" students who excel nor one of the "regular guys?" Would he become one of the lower rung of the junior high social class? I was concerned about what low self-esteem would produce in this energized teenager. All of this worried me.

All through sixth grade, we were paying for the services of a private tutor. Ben's work on reading skills had begun positively, but lately he had seemed to be resistant to instruction. The oppositional defiance, so common with bipolar children, was making itself evident. Ben often worked against the people who were trying to help him. I saw this very clearly when I helped him with his homework. The tutor decided Ben needed a break from her instruction. I took a look at what I could do to help prepare Ben for seventh grade.

My daughter, Caroline, had been in that same school four years earlier, so I had some clues about what Ben would face. I knew he would be taking a health class in which he would write three research papers. For Ben, this would be an overwhelming task. Failure to do these papers at all, or doing them poorly, would be especially unfortunate for Ben because he was genuinely interested in the functions of the body, health, and healing. When Garry had his gallbladder surgery, it was Ben who showed more interest in the surgery than anyone else. He had many questions for the surgeon, who in turn showed an interest in him.

I did not want Ben to have a discouraging experience in health. Further, since I had heard so many positive things about the class from Caroline, I wanted Ben to have a good experience as well. I also wanted to continue his use of the computer as an aid to doing acceptable looking school work, so I hit upon the idea of having him work on these three papers during the summer. He could have three months to learn how to do a research paper; he would use the computer, and he would learn to find his numerous errors and correct them without erasures and mess. Ben would do actual assignments he could hand in during the upcoming year! I hoped he would feel he had a head start for 7th grade and feel more prepared for what he was to face. I hoped it would improve his self-confidence.

While working on the papers, his old problem with cognitive looseness was painfully evident. The disorganized narrative and the tendency to make illogical leaps made his ideas hard to follow. I spent a lot of time working on the papers with Ben to help him produce something that made sense and gave him some help in how to spot his errors. These papers were a big project for Ben and me. We were both frustrated by the time we finished the last of the three papers at the end of August.

The research papers were our effort to improve Ben's reading and writing skills. To address my other concern, that of Ben handling himself with older peers, we looked at Aikido, one of the martial arts. We chose it because of the principle of this form of self-defense. Its aim is the neutralization of an attacker, rather than aggression. The goal of Aikido is not to hurt someone else but to disarm and escape attack. Aikido is suited to all ages and body types, so it would be ideal to help a smaller student to defend himself against a larger one.

I felt it was important for Ben to learn a non-violent, non-aggressive means of coping with possible harassment or intimidation from the ninth graders who were bigger and stronger. I hoped the Aikido training might also help him feel more confident about handling whatever situation arose. The classes were available at the local YMCA. Ben took lessons that summer and enjoyed this mental and physical training program. (Recently I learned that martial arts are an especially good sport for students with ADHD.)

When seventh grade approached, I held my breath and crossed my fingers. It turned out to be a pleasant surprise. Much of seventh grade went well for Ben. He was taking a low dosage of imipramine at bedtime, which seemed to help him sleep and feel more alert the next day. He arose each morning with his alarm clock, showered, got his own breakfast and caught the 7:10 bus. This was quite a switch for us. All six years of elementary school we had to coax him out of bed, get out the clothes he was to wear, make his breakfast for him, and drive him to school at 8:45. Ben in seventh grade was like a different kid.

He liked all his teachers, but he especially admired his math teacher. Although math was a struggle for him, he felt comfortable in the structured environment this teacher established in his classroom. Band was another surprise for us. Getting him to practice was not the problem I thought it was going to be, because playing the trombone was one of Ben's talents. He had good things to say about all of his teachers.

He enjoyed his health class, and since his three research papers were already done, he could relax knowing things would turn out fairly well for him. Ben's health teacher gave each student a questionnaire to fill out that gave parents some insights into their children. The title on the top read: "These are some things about school and you and me." I think it gives some fairly revealing looks into Ben's thinking. A careful reading of his responses shows the social isolation he felt, his concern over his grades, and his need for us to understand his struggle.

1. The class I enjoy the most is <u>Band</u>, because <u>it's cool.</u>

2. The class I learn the most in is <u>Band</u>, because <u>it's cool</u>.

3. I have to work the hardest in <u>Math</u>, because <u>teacher</u>

4. People I like to or would like to spend time with in school are <u>me</u>.

5. This year, I hope I can or will <u>Pass 7 grade</u>

6. A goal of some kind <u>get good grades</u>

7. As my parents or guardians, you have helped me <u>Pick up my towels in my</u> <u>room (Ha) (ha)</u>

8. As my parents or guardians, I would like you to/or need from you, <u>your money, your car and your pitty.</u> (pity misspelled)

9. My feelings about you are <u>your prity</u> (pretty is misspelled and then crossed out and replaced by)<u> really cool</u>.

The fact that our son appreciated our efforts to help him gave us motivation to hang in there when the going got tough.

That year Ben developed an interest in ham radio and wanted us to buy him one. We hesitated. A ham radio is an expensive item, and I did not want to spend a lot of money for what might turn out to be a passing whim. After some thought, we made an agreement. Since we had to forego our yearly family vacation to Florida at Christmas time because of a special event for our daughter, we would give Ben the money we would have spent on an airplane ticket for him had we gone. He would have the first half of what was needed to buy the radio. If he was still serious about buying the radio when next Christmas rolled around, we would give him the other half of the money. I gave the money to him in $1 bills along with a lock box to keep it in. I thought saving the money in that form would be a good discipline for him. He liked the arrangement and he was very careful with the money.

Seventh grade was also the year Ben began to see a pediatric cardiologist. At his Mayo Clinic evaluation in sixth grade, the doctors had found Ben's cholesterol level was 223. Since 200 is the upper limits of what can still be considered within the normal range for an adult, Ben's level was considered extremely high cholesterol for a boy his age. Re-testing at age twelve showed Ben's level was 240. The pediatrician suggested he see the pediatric cardiologist who came to our town bimonthly. The specialist recommended Ben increase his exercise, decrease the fat content of his diet, and try to lose some weight.

Throughout Ben's childhood, I had tried a number of methods to help him do precisely that. He would lose weight for a time, but as with most people who "battle the bulge," he would quickly regain any losses. Since my husband also had elevated cholesterol, we decided this time we would begin a family campaign to change eating patterns. The emphasis was not on weight but on the reduction of both Garry's and Ben's cholesterol.

One of my sisters had died of heart failure at the age of thirteen, so I knew it is possible for a young person to have a serious cardiac condition requiring careful treatment. There was also a history of heart disease in Garry's family. We took Ben's

240 cholesterol level seriously. That winter and the early spring of Ben's seventh grade, he lost 13 pounds and his cholesterol dropped 40 points.

The very last weeks of school, Ben began doing something he had never done before: he started going to the neighborhood park with friends. I felt uncomfortable about what he was doing there, and although I was glad to see him interacting with other young people, I did not get the impression they were doing positive things. With summertime coming up, I began to wonder what kind of trouble Ben might get into during his idle hours.

What positive activities might he have to occupy himself? His grades had been good enough in his first year of junior high, so we felt he deserved some reinforcement by getting a break from school work. But he needed something to occupy his time. We decided to emphasize other types of work. Ben agreed to do some work at home and for our family business, a group home, by doing lawn mowing, painting and house cleaning.

What a relief it was coming home to a house cleaned by my son rather than messed up by him! The house did not get as messy when Ben, who created the lion's share of the messes, realized it would be part of his job to clean it up. The painting and lawn mowing he did at our group home was as good as many of our other employees had done.

But Ben's work schedule did not keep Ben from getting into mischief. I remember one summer day when something he said gave me a clue. I had asked him how things were going, and his response was, "I'm trying it all, Mother." I knew one of the things he was doing in the park with his friends was smoking, but I wondered if he was not also experimenting with other substances. There was an isolated incident with experimentation with alcohol but no evidence of any drug use. After Ben's death, I had some frank talks with his friends about this, and they were quite insistent that Ben had not been experimenting with drugs. So, to my knowledge, his "trying it all" may have consisted only of chewing and smoking tobacco and a single bout with alcohol.

In July, Garry and I attended a conference in Chicago. Garry went to the first week of the conference, and I attended the second week. We went at different times so we would only be gone from Ben for the weekend between the meetings. While in Chicago we contacted an old friend, a psychiatrist who is an expert in the diagnoses of depression. Our friend suggested that Ben's genetic background would make him a likely candidate to have bipolar (manic depressive) illness. I asked him for a treatment referral somewhere in our state. He told me to send him the report from Mayo and he would contact someone at University Hospital in Minneapolis.

After returning from Chicago, I told Ben we thought his depression was bipolar illness. I also mentioned my suspicions about his "trying it all" with his friends. The treatment for his illness would start as soon as the referral process was complete. Until then, we wanted to help Ben avoid any experimentation with street drugs and any other trouble he might be getting into. Specifically, I asked Ben to stop going to the park with his friends. He promised to try to do this but said he would need some help saying "No" to these kids. I volunteered to act as a "door guard" telling these kids either Ben was unavailable, or was busy working, or was not allowed out of the house. For the most part, I could be careful about the exact wording of what I told them and manage not to lie. But at that point I did not hesitate to do what was needed to break his connection with them. I had always taught my children to be helpful or kind to others when they came to the door, so my playing the heavy took some getting used to for all of us.

It was about this time that a new friend came into Ben's life. At first I was a little leery of Ben's new friendship, but it was not long before I began to hope this boy might be a true friend to him. He was two years older than Ben and an outdoors enthusiast. He shared Ben's interest in fishing and hunting, and he had a job at a nearby stable. One day Ben accompanied him to work where they did the chores together. Ben came home sore after spending four hours of shoveling out the stalls but said he had a great time. Ben decided he wanted a job at the stables more than anything else in the world. I advised him to do some volunteer work. He would learn a lot about the horses and the operation of the stables, and then when one of the other employees quit their job the owner would see the advantage of hiring Ben.

His first reaction was negative. Although he loved the work, not getting paid seemed unreasonable to him. Ben liked being with his friend; he loved being with the horses. He actually did not mind shoveling out the stalls, so in the end Ben volunteered at the stables quite often. The owner of the stables liked Ben and was friendly toward this unpaid worker.

During that summer, Ben learned a little Morse code in preparation for the ham radio. We had a tall aerial installed for Ben which could be used both for the ham, when he got it, and for the CB he had borrowed. Ben always enjoyed talking with adults and made quite a number of CB buddies.

We hoped we were keeping Ben occupied and out of trouble while waiting for treatment to begin, but towards the end of the summer Ben had the one incident with alcohol I mentioned earlier. One morning when we tried to get him up to mow a lawn, we discovered he was drunk. Later, we searched his room and found two pint bottles: one empty and one almost full. His words, "I'm trying it all, Mother" came back to me. Garry and I confronted him with what we had found. We wanted to know what was going on. "I'm a kid. I'm experimenting with things. Didn't you want to try things when you were young?" was his explanation.

I tried to get some perspective on his response. His comment made me think about my own drinking when I was young. For the last twenty years, my drinking has consisted of a glass of wine two or three times a year, but when I was younger I drank much more. My youthful drinking was associated with social events, and its purpose was to become less inhibited, thus allowing me to have more fun at parties and dances. The idea of Ben, at age thirteen, drinking alone in his room to the point of getting sick did not seem to be normal drinking behavior. It did not have anything at all to do with having fun. We had some more frank talks about his possible illness, and Ben told us he was at last willing to see a psychiatrist.

As summer drew to an end, I was encouraged that Ben had a new friend and was becoming involved in outdoor activities. I was impatient for the referral process to speed up so Ben could start seeing someone for further evaluation and treatment. I was concerned about his impulsive, experimental behaviors, and I was cognizant that we were running out of time with Ben. Up to this point, Ben had always been willing to cooperate with us. He would soon get into the age in which parental defiance is to be expected.

Eighth Grade

I n September, some of the weight Ben lost the previous spring was still off. He had also grown a few inches during the summer and he did not look overweight. He felt good about his body image as school began. Depressed young people have a tendency to either overeat or undereat, and the food issue was a constant problem for Ben. He had marked fluctuations in his weight. In the middle of May, when Garry and he were conscientiously working to reduce cholesterol, Ben had gotten down to 152 pounds. By early November he was up to 178.

Some of that weight gain may have occurred during the summer when Ben was alone in the house and it was harder for us to monitor him. He had difficulty controlling his own eating without someone around to encourage him to eat properly. At Ben's first appointment with the psychiatrist in mid-October, he weighed 170. At his follow-up appointment, he was up to 178. Part of the eight pound gain in those three weeks may have been due to lithium. This medication, a natural element, is like salt, and is helpful to many people with bipolar illness. But it can also cause increased appetite. Unfortunately for Ben, he was caught between the complications of management of depressive illness and the management of his weight, a risk factor in cardiovascular problems.

Before his first appointment with the psychiatrist in October, Ben and I had a talk. He looked forward to telling the psychiatrist what was really going on in his life. This adolescent who had so vehemently refused to see anyone two years earlier was now serious about dealing with his problems. I was proud of him.

Ben's psychiatrist specializes in working with adolescents, and she was able to establish a rapport with him almost immediately. After talking with him alone, she asked us to join them. The plan was for Ben to see her every three weeks and for him to start medication. He could either start on an antidepressant only or the lithium only. Since Ben's genetic background indicated bipolar illness and lithium is the most important medication for the condition, it was agreed to start with the lithium and add the antidepressant later if needed.

At home, Garry and I continued to encourage Ben to occupy himself with activities that he enjoyed. Ben volunteered at the stables each weekend that autumn. He also showed enthusiasm for hunting. With the approach of hunting season, Ben needed to take a gun safety class if he was to go hunting with his friend, Garry, and Garry's friend. Ben signed up for a night class offered by community schools. He did some studying and managed to pass the gun safety tests.

Shooting a gun was another thing Ben was good at. He had started to do some trap shooting with my husband and seemed to have some talent for it. The end of the gun safety class coincided with the beginning of hunting season. The hunting foursome consisted of the two boys and two men. Something about the two older men sharing a hunting experience with the boys struck me as just the right kind of thing for the guys to do together.

Ben was seeing his therapist every three weeks. He genuinely liked her and felt these visits and the medication were helpful to him. In late November or early December the decision was made to add an antidepressant because Ben was still experiencing depression even with the lithium. What antidepressant should Ben use? Psychiatrists have found that if a particular medication or combination of medications work well for one member of a family, they often work well for other members of the family. This is logical since family members often have similar body chemistry, and they typically have similar reactions to medications. This is especially true with illnesses that have a strong genetic factor. My husband had been taking Prozac since January of 1988 and had been doing well with the combination of it and the lithium he had started late in August of that same year. Ben's biological make-up probably would be similar to Garry's, and since Prozac had worked well for Garry, it was a logical choice.

When talking about the Prozac, the subject of potential side effects was raised. Prozac did not have many of the side effects that other antidepressants like the tricyclics have. But Ben's psychiatrist did inform us that Prozac can trigger mania in persons with bipolar (manic-depressive) illness. Another temporary side effect for some people taking Prozac is weight loss. We were already familiar with this from the experience my husband had with the medication. Garry started taking Prozac soon after the medication came on the market, and he originally shed some of his unwanted weight. Garry still experienced problems with mood swings when taking Prozac alone. When he began taking the lithium he stabilized and so did his appetite. The lithium may have increased Garry's appetite, but we can not be sure.

Ben started with one capsule of Prozac a day and then went to two capsules daily after his next visit with the psychiatrist in mid December. Two capsules a day is the usual dosage for that medication. Shortly after starting the two Prozac a day, Ben became more impulsive.

I remember the psychiatrist saying Prozac can trigger manic behavior in some patients with bipolar illness. I called her on the phone saying, "I think we may have produced mania in this manic-depressive." I described what seemed to be some increased impulsive, unstable behaviors. She could not be certain the medication had actually caused heightened impulsivity. When one is dealing with an impulsive kid, it is very difficult to know exactly how to proceed. Medications which help raise depressed mood may also raise the type of behavior one is prone to display whenever you feel energetic. When Ben was depressed, he did not have much energy, but when less depressed, his energies would not necessarily channel themselves into orderly, constructive activity. With his ADHD compounding the bipolar illness, his impulsive behaviors had the potential for being challenging for both him and us.

The psychiatrist did not suggest any change in medication, but instead recommended Ben begin to see a therapist in our own town while continuing to see her for the monitoring of the medicine. Since our city did not have a psychiatrist who specializes in child or adolescent mental illness, I did not know whom I could take Ben to see, but I took her suggestion under consideration.

In January, I did take Ben to a local psychiatrist. During the interview, Ben and I gave her some background information about his problem and what we had been doing about it. The woman seemed genuinely willing to help us, but in the car on the way home Ben made it very clear he was not interested at all in being in therapy with her. Since he showed such resistance to the efforts of the local therapist, there was no reason to continue with therapy. Ben's psychiatrist concurred with this decision.

In early February, Ben got his report card. He received an incomplete in math, indicating he was continuing to have difficulty completing assignments. I had assumed the medications Ben was taking might help with his concentration and thus help him function more effectively in school, but this did not seem to be the case. Each night we would ask Ben if he had homework. Some nights he would tell us he did, and he would spend time in his room doing it. Other times he would tell us "No," and we believed him. This incomplete made me conclude Ben had been lying to us. I did not know how much I could trust my son or what to believe. I wondered how I could continue to help him work out his difficulties when I could not be sure he was being honest with me. How could I help him stay on track when I did not have the slightest way of knowing where he was with his assignments? How much of this was ADHD, how much of this was depression, and how much of this was just manipulative behavior?

I felt Ben needed to be punished in a way that would motivate him to assume responsibility. I decided to put the new ham radio he received for Christmas into our closet. He would get it back in six weeks, the end of the next grading period, if he had no incompletes. I also told him he needed to be careful not to alienate us. We were his parents who loved him; we were more committed to him than anyone else was likely to be. We needed to be able to trust him so we could help him when he got into trouble. Ben was more careful about getting his assignments done, and his ham radio was returned.

I can not remember exactly when Ben's nosebleeds began, but it was sometime that winter. In an article in the June, 1991 issue of Atlantic Monthly, Dr. Philip C. Kendall was interviewed about his work with children with depression and anxiety. A client was mentioned who had frequent headaches and nosebleeds. I found the article interesting. Did Ben's depression and anxiety have something to do with those twice a day nosebleeds?

When they began, I thought it might have something to do with wintertime dryness. Although the humidity in our house is adequate, I put a vaporizer in Ben's bedroom. When this did not help to reduce the frequency of the nosebleeds, I called our family doctor. He recommended coating the inside of Ben's nose with Vaseline, and to continue with the vaporizer. One day Ben had a particularly bad nosebleed and we made an appointment with an ear-nose-and-throat specialist. The doctor cauterized the nose, but Ben still had a nosebleed later that very night. A few weeks later, we went for a second visit to the ENT specialist, but it still did not resolve the problem.

During the winter. Ben continued his interest in horses. He did not go out to the stable as often as he had in the fall, but he did get there most weekends. As springtime approached, Ben again told me how desperately he wanted a job at the stables so he could spend more time with the horses. I got the idea of signing him up for riding lessons. He would have lots of contact with horses as well as learn about them. I hoped he would feel less helpless about waiting to be offered a job at the stables.

I saw these riding lessons as potentially helpful to Ben in a number of ways. First, working with horses was one of Ben's talents. I wanted to encourage him in anything that he was good at. Second, since he had expressed a strong desire to do work with horses, I wanted him to see that there is not just one way to get what you want in life. If one thing does not work out exactly as you planned, there are other possibilities that may turn out even better in the long run. Although a job at the stable might be good, would not riding lessons and having his own horse actually be better? Finally, since he only saw his therapist once every three weeks, would not riding every day be in it's own way therapeutic? Not only would it do him some good emotionally, but the added exercise would be helpful in lifting his mood.

The lessons were being offered through the same community schools programs as the gun safety class he had taken in fall. The more Ben thought about the lessons the more excited he became. One day he asked to see my copy of the enrollment slip so he could check the exact time and location of the first class. I took it from my purse. When he looked at the piece of paper, he saw that I had signed up for a one night class on adolescent suicide. Ben asked, "What's that for?" I explained to him how a friend of mine had called me about it. She was planning to go, and she wondered if I would be interested in it as well. My friend knew I was concerned about Ben's depression. His response to me was a very patronizing, "Really mother, I'm beyond that."

When Ben started therapy, he had mentioned how he had once held a gun to his head. At that time, his therapist had cautioned us to make sure Ben did not have hunting equipment in his room. We took this seriously and locked up the guns. She also did not want us to completely prohibit Ben's enjoyment of shooting since it seemed like such a positive way for him to spend time with his dad and his friend. Shooting was something he was good at and loved to do. Ben needed more enjoyable activities in his life, not less. We tried to make sure Ben's handling of a gun was supervised.

Our concerns in fall and winter about safety were prudent, but what Ben seemed to be saying now was that the danger had passed. With someone like Ben, however, one could not be sure. Ben felt he was emotionally better and beyond any danger of seriously hurting himself. As the spring approached, Ben did seem to be getting along better with other people. He was taking lithium and the anti-depressant (Prozac) and seeing his therapist. Sometimes when his dad would pick him up after school Ben would be in a good mood, saying he had a great day. We were becoming closer as a family now that we could enjoy Ben's company. The four of us would have pleasant talks in the evening or have fun playing a game. Doing things like this had never been possible when Ben was overly sensitive and easily frustrated. As the highs and lows of his mood swings leveled off, he seemed to be operating in the middle range, which allowed all of us to relax and enjoy having him around.

In April, Ben started his riding lessons. He got along famously with the instructor. Ben liked adults, and the teacher was quite taken by this fourteen year old who seemed mature for his age. By his second lesson, I was already inquiring into the possibility of leasing a horse for the summer.

Everything seemed to be going well for Ben. He was settling down emotionally, he had hobbies, and he was enjoying himself. I wondered how much longer Ben would need to continue to see his psychiatrist. I hoped he could finish out the calendar year with her and then try decreasing the visits, especially during the snow-filled winter months. My perceptions of Ben as more stable may have been shared by his therapist, for in early May, she decided to discontinue the lithium on a trial basis. This is often done to discover if a medication is necessary and effective in treatment. She did not want to continue to give a medication for a long period of time without knowing for sure that Ben really needed it. Remember, from October to December of l988 he had only been on the lithium. From December to May of l989 he had both the antidepressant, Prozac, and the lithium. Ben was looking forward to the summer and his horse. The summer seemed like a safe time to try a reduction in medications. We would be able to see how Ben would be on the anti-depressant alone.

But several months earlier, Ben had expressed to me his fears about being taken off lithium. He felt it stabilized him and he did not want to stop taking it. When this reduction was presented, Ben said he would go along with it because it was a trial and he could go back on it. I did not have any objections to the reduction. If Ben could be helped by taking only the anti-depressant alone, I would be thrilled. After all, the lithium may have been a factor in his latest weight gain. I knew how much this boy had constantly fought the battle with the bathroom scale.

The first week of the medication reduction, Ben was to go from the three tablets of lithium per day down to two. That first week everything seemed to be going along fine. I began to think maybe we were wrong about Ben's need for lithium. It was also during that week I bought Ben a saddle for the horse we were leasing for the summer. It was one of the nicest experiences I can remember. His riding teacher had come across the saddle at a garage sale. She told us about it and said if we were interested in buying it, we could bring it out to her house and give it a test ride to see if it fit the horse and was comfortable for Ben. We followed her suggestion. The saddle was fine and we were thrilled with the purchase. In the car coming back home with it, Ben saw some young people his age and commented, "Very few kids are as lucky as I am."

Being in a playful mood, we plotted to play a trick on Garry. We would tell my husband the used saddle did not work out but we had bought a new, expensive one at the saddle shop instead. Ben played his part of the joke perfectly, and it went without a hitch. We brought in the saddle, and then laughed as we explained how we were only kidding and got this saddle at a lower price. We all had a great time. In fact, everything that first week seemed to be going smoothly.

The second week Ben was to go from two lithium tablets down to just one. Somewhere during this week we began to see some of his old problems returning, especially his difficulty settling down at night and getting to sleep. During the end of the second week Garry was going to be out of town for a conference. While he was gone we were to have house guests. I wanted one of our guests to use Ben's bedroom, which meant he would have to make it presentable. Although he made some good-natured protests, he was in a cooperative mood and he said, "Oh well, I'll just whistle while I work." He went about doing a major overhaul to his room.

When I took in the mail, I received a notice from one of his teachers. There was a possibility Ben would fail one of his classes. As long as we were overhauling his room, I had him take out his ham radio and package it up until his classwork improved again. It did not seem as if he was getting his act together regarding completing assignments after all. When Ben went to school on Monday, he talked with his teacher, who was willing to work out a deal with him on how he could complete some work and pass the class.

On Wednesday night we talked, and Ben expressed unhappiness about school and his medication reduction. I encouraged him to tell his therapist exactly what was happening.

The following day Ben was supposed to start the third week of his lithium reductions, which meant he would completely stop taking it. Things were not going well, so I decided to put aside any further reduction and just have Ben stay at one tablet a day.

I thought about calling his therapist, but I felt I did not have anything concrete to say. Although we had noticed some difficulty with sleep, there had only been one night of total sleeplessness. Ben told me he could not stand being in school, but I was not sure what he meant. With no more than a general impression of his instability, I could not articulate anything objective. It made more sense to hold the lithium to one pill than to call the therapist with vague impressions. Although one tablet a day is not a therapeutic dose of lithium, giving the one daily pill might facilitate a quicker re-establishment of the medication at the full dosage. We would just wait until his regularly scheduled appointment the following week. Then the therapist could see Ben for herself and render a more objective opinion about recurring symptoms and his need for the lithium.

My weekend house guests came, and Ben seemed a little impulsive and hyperactive. While the rest of us went to my niece's graduation, Ben went with a friend to the horse stables. Having Ben on his own like that made me uneasy, and when I got back home I was relieved but also surprised to see him asleep in his bed.

The following Monday, Garry was home from his conference. I told him about the letter from his teacher, but by then we also knew there was a way to work out the failing grade. Ben's therapist had encouraged us to continue to expect Ben to do his work and to make some of the things he enjoyed contingent upon completion of his school work. Garry was trying to enforce the rule that Ben was not to go to the stables until, and unless, his school work was done. But it was hard to always get a reliable answer to the question: "Is your school work done?"

A limited amount of time remained in the school year for Ben to complete his assignments. He probably had not been doing all of his work for the last several months, even though many nights he would tell us his school work was complete. The end of the school year, the time for all assignments to be handed in, coincided with his lower dosages of lithium. At Ben's next appointment with his therapist, May 25, she could see Ben was not in as good a shape as he had been three weeks earlier. She told us to go ahead with the full therapeutic dosage of lithium immediately. The nervousness I experienced the previous two weeks was replaced with relief. Now that it was clear that Ben benefited from the medication, he would probably stay on three tablets for the rest of his life. I began to relax and to stop worrying about him.

Ben had been invited to a friend's home for Memorial Day weekend, so my husband and I had planned our own vacation. We could enjoy pursuing some of our own personal creative activities. We remarked to each other how this was the first time we could enjoy a whole weekend at our own house, on our own, since the children were born. Our daughter had left for a three week trip to Germany, and Ben was away with a friend for the weekend. We were childless and felt like newlyweds. Stopping by at Garry's sister's house while out for a walk, we reflected that we might not mind an empty nest when it came in four or five years.

On Sunday night we picked up Ben, who had a great time with his friend. He had helped their family with a building project at their home on a lake. The next morning, May 29, Ben slept late, and had his riding lesson in the afternoon. When we got there, I reminded his instructor that Thursday was June 1. We planned to be at her house after school on Thursday to ride, since it was the first official day of the lease of her horse. Ben grabbed his new saddle from the back of our car and went off to his lesson.

When he came back one hour later, his teacher expressed concern over an injury to Ben's leg. The other rider's horse had bolted and rammed up against Ben's horse. Ben came close to being pinned under the weight of both horses which would have fallen on top of him. Luckily, both riders had handled the horses fairly well and Ben's leg had only been squeezed between the horse and the wall. Everyone had been a bit shaken by the accident.

Ben had another near miss a week earlier with his bike. When riding home from the stables he had nearly been hit by a car. Looking back now, these incidents seem like a premonition of things to come. Tuesday, May 30th, Ben went to school. When he got home, he wanted to go to the stables. Garry asked Ben if he had his work done, and he told us it was finished. Ben then went to the stables with a new friend who was interested in training horses. The following day was May 31.

May 31, 1989

O n May 31, 1989, my son killed himself. Our much loved, very loving, difficult boy was gone. As I stood there looking down at Ben's body, my own body became infused with a message that said, "This was supposed to happen this day." I struggled to put into my head the knowledge I felt in my body; I desperately tried to make some sense out of it. Why was this supposed to happen? Why was it supposed to happen this particular day?

I had been all too painfully aware of Ben's depression, but I never thought he would take his own life. Nor did I see any reason for him to do such a thing on that particular day. It seemed in most respects to be a day like any other day. He had gone to school as usual. We had gone to work as usual. Nothing was out of the ordinary.

When I was a child my parents taught me that the day you are to die is established for you from the time of your birth. They said nothing in the world can be done to alter the appointed hour. They used to say, "When your time is up, your time is up." So when the powerful message came to me, filling me from head to toe stating, "This was supposed to happen this day," it was a type of validation of their teaching.

In the weeks and months that followed I often wondered what the purpose was of his dying on that particular day. Although I have thought about it much and have come up with several possibilities, as of this writing I do not have a clear answer to this question. I do, however, sense that something deep within myself and my husband was helping to prepare us for Ben's death. This preparation came to us in three separate forms: dreams, intuition, and anxiety.

Three or four days before my son died, I had a powerful dream that made a strong impression on me. It was very simple: I had breast cancer and was going to die. When I awoke I knew this was important and I gave it careful consideration. I wondered if it was a statement about my health or if it was symbolic of something else. I thought about the feeling of the dream; the impression it produced was fear. I awoke feeling terribly frightened about an upcoming death. I remembered thinking: this dream does not make any sense to me. I am feeling frightened by death, but I am not afraid to die. I did not know the full meaning of the dream, but my initial interpretation was of a fear of death.

Looking back at it now, I can guess at the symbolism. One of the associations I make to the symbol of breasts is "mothering and nurturing." I believe the dream helped prepare me for my son's death. Why does our unconscious find it necessary to prepare us for tragedies? I do not know, but it must serve a useful purpose. When Ben's death came I was understandably devastated by his suicide and surprised by it, but on another level I was prepared.

In the months since his death I have learned that when someone dies by suicide, the survivors are often filled with "If only..." regrets. I have read many stories written by the parents of children and young adults who took their own lives. In describing the last days of their child's life, these parents often say "If only I had taken him (or her) to a therapist when I saw this behavior, I might have saved him (or her)." Although being in therapy does significantly reduce the risk of suicide, many depressed people commit suicide while under treatment for their condition. It is not clear to me that anything in the world can circumvent the appointed hour of one's death.

The day of Ben's death began like any other. It had been a happy time for me because I had taken some vacation time to work on a writing project. This day, however, I found myself working frantically and feeling anxious. I told my husband, Garry, of my high anxiety level when I saw him at lunch. I remember feeling like I was jumping right out of my skin, and I could not figure out why. The project seemed to be working out well and I was pleased with the results. I could not figure out where this anxiety was coming from and why there was so much of it. Garry suggested I stop working for a while, but I did not see how this would reduce my anxiety, so I continued working.

Garry also had a disturbing dream that day. In his dream he saw an image of guns pointed at someone's head. It was either his own head or Ben's; the dream was not clear. When Garry awoke, he temporarily forgot the dream and only later in the day was he able to recall it. Garry remembers feeling tired and out of sorts that morning but he could not understand why.

At 3:10 Ben came home from school as usual. I was concerned about his eating habits. Ben's after school snacks were consisting of high sugar foods. We tried hard to steer him away from this eating pattern, but he always returned to it. Ben was gaining weight from eating too much junk food. I had ignored the situation for some time but decided I should not let him continue the behavior. I went to have a talk with him.

He was in one of the back garages and I said, "Ben, you have got to stop doing what you are doing. You have got to stop eating junk and start eating nutritious food." He responded angrily saying, "Stop treating this as if it were a crime."

A few minutes later we were both in the house and this time I was angry. I said "Ben, you have to start taking care of your health." We had a short conversation. I expressed my concern that he devise some sort of plan for taking better care of himself. Ben became upset and weepy. His response to me was, "A lot you would care if something happened to me." His reaction, although understandable, made me even angrier. After all, if I did not care about him, what was I doing trying to help him? What had I been doing all these years but trying to help him? I said, "That's not true." My fears for his health turned to anger at times when he did not seem to be taking care of himself. This was one of those days when I was especially worried and when his anger triggered my own.

I had made previous arrangements to go to dinner with some friends, so I left shortly after our conversation. My husband stayed to talk with Ben who was angry with me and critical of himself. He made deprecating comments that began with "Just look at me."

I think Ben was beginning to despair about his weight. Every time his weight would stabilize or decrease he would feel hopeful, but each time it took a leap forward he became discouraged. I had tried to encourage him by telling him about research on habit control which suggests that people who persist in trying different approaches ultimately become successful. I told him he should not become discouraged just because he had not yet found a system which worked for him. But perhaps Ben was beginning to wonder if things were ever going to work out for him.

As Garry and Ben talked, the conversation turned to the subject of his homework. My husband asked Ben what he had to do. Ben said he had a lot of catching up to do and he could not do it. Garry encouraged him to give it a try. Soon after their talk, Garry had to leave the house to attend an evening meeting for work. He promised to check in on Ben later to see how he was coming along with his school work. Garry left the room to get Ben a can of pop, and when he returned, Ben was fairly calm. He asked what time Garry would be returning, and Garry told him it would probably be sometime around 7:15.

My friends decided to come back to my house to play a few hands of cards. We arrived home about the same time Garry was returning from his meeting. Garry informed me that Ben was missing. This had never happened before. We usually knew where Ben was. Because of his depression and anxiety, the only places he felt comfortable were at home, at the homes of a few close friends, at the horse stable where he volunteered, and at our family business -- a group home for handicapped adults. Since he was not at any of those places and he had never been missing before, we did not have the slightest idea of where to start looking for him.

When I asked if Ben's bike was missing, Garry went to our garage and found it indeed was gone. Ben never went off on his bike as many kids do; he felt uncomfortable out on his own. To take his bike and go to a friend's house would have been unusual behavior for him. Both my husband and I were feeling frightened, but we hoped Ben's absence only meant he had been defiant and had gone out rather than doing his school work. We had taught both of our children to leave a note on the kitchen table if they had gone someplace unexpectedly, but there was no reassuring note on the table. Garry and I decided to take a "wait and see" attitude towards Ben's disappearance. I started to play cards with my friends, and Garry went to mow the lawn. I was worried about Ben, but I tried to concentrate on the game. I told myself, "Well you had better start getting used to this. Lots of parents of teenagers do not know where their kids are every minute, and they do not know everything they do."

The topic of conversation at the card table turned to kids. One of my friends took out a newspaper article she was carrying with her. (Later she told me she did not know why she felt compelled to have me read this article; she just knew she should share it with me.) The article was addressed to parents who feel guilty about how their children behave and try to figure out what they did wrong. The author described how, paradoxically, some children with neglectful or abusive parents manage to overcome many disadvantages and became productive citizens, while other children with parents who did everything in their power to help them have difficulty managing their lives. The article emphasized the importance of genetics in explaining behavior. Persons with a fortunate genetic endowment can make use of the opportunities they are presented with, while those with unfortunate genetic make-up have difficulties no matter how supportive and helpful the families are.

As I read it I could barely keep back the tears. Sometime during those last few minutes I began to have a strong fear something terrible had happened. My guess was we would find our son in one of the back garages. He had been going out there often during the last weeks, and I feared we would find him in our old Volkswagen with his wrists cut.

While I played cards, my husband was cutting the lawn. At exactly the same time that I suspected Ben had hurt himself, Garry also had the premonition Ben might be dead. While mowing the grass he suddenly recalled the dream he had had earlier in the day in which there were guns pointed at someone's head. Garry stopped the lawn mower. His intuition also told him he would find Ben in the back garage. He thought Ben would be there hanging. Garry went to the back garage, but Ben was not there.

Garry then went down to check his studio in the basement of our group home next door. He saw the locked door had been kicked in, and Ben was lying on the floor. In the confused emotions of the moment, Garry thought if he hugged Ben and kissed him, somehow he could bring him back to life. If he could show Ben how much he loved him, Garry thought he could change things.

While playing cards with my friends, I heard someone staggering up the back steps. The sound was vaguely like the noise Ben made when he came bounding home. I hoped Garry had found Ben loafing and had sent him back to his room to do some schoolwork. As worried as I had been about Ben, I could not have cared less about his homework. I was so relieved he was coming back home that I literally jumped out of my chair, fully intending to embrace him and tell him how glad I was to see him. Instead, the sound was Garry stumbling in the back door, half fainting or in shock, stating "It's Ben!"

"Should I call 911?" I asked. He replied, "Yes." As I lifted the phone to call, Garry said he was going back to the studio. One of my friends volunteered to make the phone call so I could follow my husband. I told Garry I was coming, and he cried, "Don't come!" But I knew no one in the world could prevent me from seeing my son. Operating on instinct, I knew that if I did not see Ben as he was then, I might regret it for the rest of my life.

I followed Garry as he went back to his studio. Ben's body was lying on the floor. He had shot himself in the head. I felt very detached when I saw him. Feeling detached and numb is a fairly common reaction, I later learned. Perhaps it is the protection we need in an overwhelming situation like this.

For several reasons, I will always be grateful I saw Ben when I did. First of all, I received the very clear message "This was supposed to happen this day." I am not sure this would have come to me on such a deep and profound level except in the immediate presence of my son's body. Secondly, in my son's case, the damage done by the bullet was hidden from us when we looked at Ben lying on his stomach. If I had not seen him there myself I am afraid my imagination would have created a image far more horrifying than reality. Finally, with the two of us there with our son I turned to my husband and asked, "Do you blame me for this?" My husband answered "No," and said it in a way that made me know he meant it. Garry and I got it clear from the beginning that neither of us blamed the other.

I could have decided to blame myself for Ben's death. It was I who had spoken to him about his eating habits, producing his angry reaction and creating an argument between us. It was partly my attempt to discourage overeating which served as the trigger for his destructive behavior. Although my actions would not have triggered suicidal behavior in a child without a bipolar (manic-depressive) illness, it could in a youngster with that disease. Dr. Popper, a noted psychiatrist, described the anger and potentially destructive behaviors of bipolar kids in this way: Bipolar children may exhibit severe temper tantrums, approaching psychotic degrees of disorganization and releasing manic quantities of physical and emotional energy, sometimes with violence and property destruction. The major destructiveness of bipolar children...tends to occur in anger....The 'trigger' for temper tantrums for...bipolar children (is) limit-setting (e.g., a parental 'No.').

There is an important distinction   between triggering something and causing something. Ben's bipolar illness was the cause of his suicide. Twenty percent of people with this condition eventually kill themselves.   As I mentioned in the introduction, Ben had several depressive conditions and a learning problem. The combination of these conditions put him at high risk for suicide.   The trigger for his death probably was the pressures of unfinished school work and my conversation about his eating patterns. Neither my motherly concern for his physical health nor Garry's request that he try to do some of his homework are to blame for his death.   They may have been a trigger, but not a cause. Garry's statement that he did not blame me for the suicide has helped tremendously to decrease any guilt I might have chosen to carry relating to my son's self-destructive behavior.

Garry and I were with Ben's body for only a minute or so when the police arrived. They allowed us to stay with the body for a time while they made some initial inquiries. After a while, they said it was time to leave the scene. We went to another part of the basement for more extensive questioning as to the details of the incident.

At one point I was called upstairs because my sister-in-law had come to the house to find out why the 911 squad was there. I informed her of the suicide, that I was basically O.K., but Garry might be going into shock. When I returned to the basement, the officer was also becoming concerned about Garry. The person who finds the body often has an additional burden to bear. Since it was evening, the police advised us to go to the hospital for some attention. He offered to drive us: I was grateful because I did not think it was safe for us to drive.

We were at the hospital for approximately an hour. Shortly after our arrival, one of Garry's best friends arrived to see if he could help. Our friend was willing to spend the night with us, at our home. As Garry's condition stabilized we left the hospital. When we arrived home, I knew I would not be able to sleep. I wanted to rest, but I knew Garry and I would feel alone in our bedroom. I put on a sweat shirt and sweat pants, brought pillows and quilts into the living room, and we spent the night there. In that big, open, living area of our home we rested and talked, but did not sleep.

I did not want to call my family in a neighboring state until the morning. By 6 a.m. I was still numb about what had happened, and I had not been able to cry. I very much wanted to call my mother and then each of my sisters and brothers to tell them the news; this ritual was very important to me.

After I completed the last call to my family, I called my friend who was with me the night before to let her know about Ben. Her intuition had already told her what had happened, and she said she would be over. She stayed with me most of the day. It was so good to be able to tell her everything that came into my mind. Having a friend who is supportive, honest, and nonjudgmental is a treasure. She let me bring up anything I wanted to say without minimizing its importance. Sometime in the afternoon I grew tired, so she left while Garry and I got a little sleep. After a brief nap we began to think of other people who should be notified, and we made more phone calls. Garry's family came over to help us get started with some of the many decisions we needed to make. Later, our minister came over to help us with some initial planning.

One of the most poignant things I recall during that first afternoon was the feeling that I desperately wanted the power to turn back the clock 24 hours and change what had happened. Although logically I knew it was impossible to do, on that day it seemed somehow it should be possible! It had only been one day. Surely there must be a way to make it Wednesday again at 3:00 rather than Thursday. If it were Wednesday again, and Ben had just come home from school, I could stop working and we could have a quiet talk. I could offer to make him a salad. Eating together, I wouldn't have gotten upset about the junk he was consuming. I could have stayed at home and had my friends over for cards rather than going out. Surely there must be some way to turn the clock back 24 hours. It could not be that hard to do! I was thinking emotionally rather than logically. Like Garry, I wanted magical power to bring my son back to life. Garry had thought he could do it by hugging Ben's lifeless body. I thought I could do it by turning back time. But neither of us possessed the magic to save our son.

We did not sleep the second night either. Garry and I spent the evening in the living room with our quilts. Somewhere in the middle of the night, it occurred to me I would never be happy again for the rest of my life. I would never again feel joy, for every potentially happy moment would be spoiled by the fact that Ben was dead. As quickly as this idea came to mind, a totally different perspective replaced it. I remembered my father, who had died eighteen years earlier. In many respects I felt closer to him now than I had when he was alive. I have chosen to have a relationship with him by appreciating all of his fine qualities, especially his wisdom. I feel I am able to sense this wisdom when I need it. I draw strength from his strength of character, his integrity. I began to realize that, after a time, this would also be possible with Ben. His bipolar illness was a great burden for him, causing an enormous amount of difficulty coping with life. But the other side of Ben was an extremely sensitive, wonderfully loving and unusually wise youngster. In my future relationship with my son, I would be able to receive the benefits of his sensitivity, as well as the love and wisdom he possessed. A question occurred to me: What more could any mother expect to receive from her son?

As daylight appeared, I remembered what the minister said about dealing with some of Ben's belongings. He told us how some people find it easier to pack up some things right away. Although I had not slept during the night, I had the energy to get up and start re-organizing Ben's room. I very much wanted it to look different. Part of the reason we were avoiding our own bedroom was because it was adjacent to Ben's room. If we were going to live in this house and sleep in our bed, we needed to change the way Ben's room looked. Garry and I dismantled Ben's makeshift desk, moved his bed to the other side of the room and put some of his things away. I wanted to take care of his room myself and then clean my own room. I felt a need to take some of the turmoil inside me and use it to put my house in order. I wanted to do many things myself, but when my niece came over to see how she could help, I was more than happy to give her the assignment of cleaning our daughter's room. Caroline, a college student, was in Germany at the time; we reached her by phone to give her the news of her brother's death.

I was not sure coming home for the funeral would be the right thing for her to do. When telling Caroline about Ben's death I made it clear she had the choice of either coming home or staying where she was. I did not want to protect her from the death or exclude her from the process, but I wanted to respect her right to deal with things in her own way and in her own time. I felt uneasy about her traveling home alone under these circumstances. I was relieved when she decided to stay where she was. It was an honest decision based on what was right for her. We decided we could have a small private ritual when she returned.

The employees of our group homes were concerned and wanted to be helpful. They concluded that the best service they could do for us was to make sure the business ran as efficiently as it could. I have always appreciated our loyal and trustworthy staff, but in times like this, I especially realized how blessed we are to have them.

Friday morning, Garry's sister and one of her friends went with us to the mortuary to make arrangements. It is amazing how many decisions one has to make at a time when they are hard to make! We first had to decide whether we wanted Ben to be buried or cremated. Whether or not we would ultimately choose to cremate Ben's body or not, I knew I wanted it embalmed. I feel strongly that it is helpful to spend a number of days with its presence in order to bring closure with the physical body and to give ourselves enough time to say good-bye. Because he was embalmed, we had some time before we would have to decide on the final disposition of his body. This was especially important to us because it gave us time to again contact our daughter in Germany to find out her wishes. Garry wants to be cremated when he dies, so we were leaning towards this for Ben as well. But we did not want to be rushed into this decision, for once made, it can not be undone.

Selecting a coffin was one of the hardest things we had to do. The funeral director knew this would be difficult for us, and tried to prepare us for it, but I do not know how anyone can be prepared for a huge room filled with coffins. Perhaps the coffins force you to realize in a deep level the reality of what has happened. It was an overwhelming experience, and I wanted to get out of there as quickly as possible.

From the funeral home we went to the church. The minister wanted to give us some time to talk about the suicide. I found this both painful and helpful. It gave us a chance to get used to talking while crying. In the months ahead, as we worked through our grief, it would be important to talk about what had happened and how we felt. We needed to learn to continue to talk while we cried. We needed to begin to feel unashamed of crying and hoped others would feel comfortable about it too. After discussing the death, the minister involved us in the planning of the funeral. I had strong opinions about the music. I wanted a lot of it: no solos, only full congregational singing. Although solos are beautiful, I did not want anyone to feel excluded at any time from participating in the process of our final farewell to Ben's spirit in song.

Everything takes longer to do than you think, and when we finally came back home my mom and one of my sisters had arrived from out of state. Some of our friends had arrived, too, and it was comforting to see them. The flood of food had also started. At the time I could not imagine ever wanting to eat again, but I also realized there would be need for all of this food as more family and friends arrived. Later that night, with Ben's room altered in appearance and my family staying with us, Garry and I finally returned to our bedroom and got at least a few hours of sleep.

We went to the mortuary on Saturday morning. We again contacted our daughter in Germany and with her help made the decision to have the body cremated and the ashes brought home in a crypt to be placed somewhere in our home. We brought some clothing for Ben, and gave them to the mortician. We made another trip to the funeral home in the afternoon to make the decision about whether to have an open or closed casket during the visitation. This was another time we did not want to be rushed and where the funeral director was very helpful. Earlier he had advised us to let them prepare the body as well as they could and then have us come in to view it before deciding on whether to have the casket open or closed. Since the last time we had seen Ben was shortly after his suicide, the mortician said it probably would be helpful to us in the weeks and months ahead to see him now in a more peaceful state. In his opinion, it would be healing for us, and I now agree with him completely.

There was some swelling of Ben's face, so he did look slightly different than he had when alive. As I looked down on his body this second time, I felt very little connection between it and my son's spirit. My sense was that this was the part Ben had discarded. I remember saying "That isn't my son. My son continues. That is only his shell." There is a lot of healing in knowing this.

Because of the slight swelling in his face, we felt everyone would feel more comfortable with a closed casket. With the coffin closed, I wanted a lot of pictures displayed along with some of the things which were important to Ben: the saddle we had bought for horseback riding, and the trombone he loved. I was glad we had two framed collections of family snapshots at our home. I had put this collection together the year before, as a Christmas present for myself and for Garry. It contained all of my favorite pictures of Ben at all stages of his life. We put these on pedestals on either side of the entrance to the casket area.

As friends gathered at our home that evening, I realize I needed to reach out to some of Ben's closest friends to see how they were reacting to his suicide. Whenever there is a sudden death, especially a suicide, there can be the feeling that maybe something could have been done to prevent it. We especially wanted to contact Ben's friends from the horse stable. We requested they come to our house because we wanted to reassure them that we cared about them, and they were not to feel responsible for Ben's death. Logically, of course, there would be no reason for them to feel responsible, but logic has little to do with this type of situation. In cases like this, most people end up feeling, "If only I would have called him that night and offered to do something with him he would not have been alone. If he wasn't alone, he probably wouldn't have killed himself." Everyone close to the deceased takes on unnecessary responsibility for the death.

The next day was Sunday. Around noontime the rest of my family arrived from out of state. Ben's depression had been unknown to them, so I explained a little about his illness. They had only known a boy who was outgoing with adults and who had a wonderful smile. Depressed young people often try to hide their pain and cope with life as best as they can. They try to overcome their illness and protect those around them from the burden of suffering. Ben's outward jovial appearance in social situations would not have led anyone to believe how terribly uncomfortable he often felt. It takes family and friends some time to accept the idea that here was a child who had a very powerful illness.

After explaining Ben's illness and our efforts to get appropriate medical attention, I found myself hungry for the first time in three days. After eating, it was time for the visitation. We had gathered still more pictures of Ben, which we put in individual plastic pages and took them to the mortuary. It felt good to see all of our friends and get all those hugs. I found the ritual associated with the funeral very helpful.

Monday was the funeral. You often read how family members experience some shame associated with a suicide death. I felt none the day of Ben's funeral. There almost seemed to be a military feel to the event, as if he were a fallen soldier. I think this came from knowing in my heart that Ben had tried his best to cope with his powerful illness, but it had overwhelmed him. It has been said that in a depressed state, the person will feel he or she is in a dark tunnel with no light on either end. I felt Ben had done the best he could for fourteen years. He had a genetically unlucky body, but within it lived a great spirit.

FOR BEN

Ben/
No answer.
Ben/
Where is that boy?

Ben has gone
a far journey.
A journey at once
familiar to all
and yet unfamiliar.

I believe this journey
ends in love.
As all things finally
end in love.
And that Ben now
knows what he could
only guess at.

Mark Arvilla
A Duluth Poet
Ben's friend

Depression in Perspective

Before focusing in on how we can help our young people with depression, it is important to start with a fundamental understanding of the nature of this condition. In the past when a young person showed signs of depression, there was an over-emphasis on looking at what parents were doing wrong or failed to do right. Not only did this often prove to be unproductive in helping the child, but it obviously would prevent most parents from viewing the young person's depression objectively.

This chapter focuses on the biological nature of depression. Important environmental factors are put in the more relevant context of overall historical terms rather than in the personal characteristics of individual families. Depression is no one's fault. Exaggerated guilt will not arise from a logical examination of truly significant factors surrounding depression.

My grief following Ben's death led me to spend a lot of time reading about suicide and depression. I discovered it is nearly impossible to predict when someone is going to attempt suicide. Consequently, prevention needs to focus on the treatment of the conditions most frequently associated with suicide, namely, depression and anxiety. Both are important, but depression is especially important because it is a factor in most suicides.

INCIDENCE OF DEPRESSION

The major obstacle to overcome in any discussion of depression is the idea that it is a rare illness. Depression is anything but rare. Although it is fairly uncommon for the condition to be fatal (only about 15% of severally depressed persons end their lives), the illness in its milder forms is both common and painful. Psychiatrist and author Dr. David Burns (1980) writes, "Depression has been called the world's number one public health problem." Various books and articles give different statistics on exactly how many people are affected by mood disorders.

This is what we are dealing with today. "A 1986 study of Minnesota high school students reveals that 39% suffer from mild to severe depression." ("Adolescent," 1986). Dr. Mark Gold (1987), biopsychiatrist and author of The Good News About Depression, writes that the findings for college students is similar to what is found in high school. Gold states, "One out of three college students will have experienced a unipolar or bipolar episode by the time he or she has graduated."

What is the rate for adults? Dr. Gerald Klerman (1984), eminent psychiatrist and author of books on interpersonal psychotherapy for depression, wrote that "Although only a small minority of individuals experiences depressive symptoms that meet the criteria of a clinical disorder, many more experience depressive moods; about 40 percent of the population report feeling depression, disappointment and unhappiness in a year."

As we begin to realize that four out of every ten people high school age and over have some level of depression, it becomes clear why depression is the number one public health problem in the world. When you develop an awareness of the symptoms of this illness, you get an understanding of what is wrong with so many of us today. You generally hear experts talk about the incidence of depression as 10 percent. That figure refers to people with severe (clinical) depression. Ten percent of our adolescent and adult population is clinically depressed, while 30 percent has milder forms of depression; which gives a total of 40 percent.

If the incidence of mild to severe depression in teens and adults is 40%, what is the rate of depression in children? It is a hard question to answer. Dr. Gold (1987, p. 282) tells us, "Twenty years ago, psychiatrists believed that depression in childhood did not and could not exist. Now experts in child health are sounding an alarm." Parents would like to believe depression is not as high for children as it is for adolescents and adults, but experts tell us children are actually the population which has seen the greatest increase in recent years.

Getting an accurate figure on the occurrence of childhood depression is currently impossible. Most depression for all age groups goes undiagnosed. We do not screen youngsters for this very common condition. Psychiatrists can only guess at the incidence of childhood depression. In their landmark book on childhood depression, Why Johnny Isn't Crying, McKnew, Cytryn and Yahrens (1983) estimate the rate of severe depression in children ranges from 5 percent to 10 percent. This estimate for children is not that different from the data on adults -- about 10 percent suffer from severe depression.

McKnew (1983) and his colleagues believe the incidence of severe depression in children to be "from three to more than six million American children," most of which "goes unrecognized and untreated." As distressing as these figures are, they do not reflect the incidence of milder forms of depression. The amount of mild depression in children may be an additional 30 percent, the same as it is for adolescents and adults. Dr. Gold (1987) makes this comment about the lack of diagnosis in children: "The terrible truth (is childhood depression) has caught psychiatrists and pediatricians by surprise."

How is it the general public and often the medical profession have not only failed to recognize the condition but also underestimate how many young people are affected by it today? One of the reasons may be that the amount of depression seems to fluctuate at different times in history and the current high rates of mood disorders have just taken everyone by surprise.

HISTORICAL PERSPECTIVE

We do not have to go very far back to see another time in our history when depression was common. The pattern after World War I is similar in some respects to the pattern experienced since World War II. The first World War was the famous war to end all wars. The Roaring Twenties which followed the victory for the Allies was a particularly optimistic time. This optimism not only gave hope for a peaceful future under a League of Nations but a time of unlimited economic opportunities. The 1929 stock market crash ushered in an end to the exaggerated optimism. Not only was there an economic depression, but the people felt depressed. Physicians and psychiatrists began to report a widespread incidence of symptoms of what they continued to call melancholia (depression). The losses people had incurred in their lives (loss of financial security, loss of work activity, perhaps loss of their home, etc.) and the dramatic changes they were then forced to make were the cause of changed mood.

Not all loss and change results in depression. It is only when loss and change feels purposeless, meaningless, and when there is little optimism for the future that depression occurs. World War II also created its share of both change and loss, but the war solved our economic depression and lifted the nation out of its psychological depression. During the war our country busily pursued purposeful, meaningful activity, something it had not been able to do during the Depression of the 1930's.

The years after the Great War were called the Fabulous Fifties, a time of economic prosperity and stability. Because U.S. factories were not bombed during the war, America was in a position to make the products needed throughout many parts of the world. It was also a time of low rates of depression and low rates of suicide.

The decade following the bombing of Hiroshima brought a gradual proliferation of weapons and the slow realization that we were living in dangerous times. Born in 1944, I grew up in the 50's and 60's and came to know it was possible for a bomb like that to fall on us as well, destroying life as we know it. Poets and artists often become alert to change before the general public. W. H. Auden's poem, The Age of Anxiety, published in 1947, captured the feeling of the later 50's. The threat of possible annihilation which the atomic age produced was constant and something we could do little about.

My daughter is a child of the 70's and 80's. When I described to her what it was like to grow up with the anxiety of the nuclear bomb, she described to me in elegant terms why we have now shifted from a post war Age of Anxiety into an Age of Depression. She says it is almost irrelevant whether or not we have a war between a few superpowers possessing nuclear weapons. Indeed, the general lessening of tension between the former communist countries and the democracies of the West has not decreased the sense of danger felt by her generation. There is no exaggerated optimism in the 90's following the end of the cold war similar to what was experienced following the other major wars of this century. She cites overpopulation, nuclear accidents, nuclear waste and a number of other problems relating to the ecology of the planet which, from her perspective, make our destruction seem inevitable.

The words she spoke to me in our kitchen are echoed in the work of psychiatrist and author, Anthony Stevens (1989). He writes:

> If we continue as we are, the possibility of nuclear catastrophe is matched only by the certainty of ecological disaster. The explosive increase in world population, infinite problems of providing enough food, the rapid growth of industrial pollution, the poisoning of the atmosphere, the oceans, lakes, and streams, the destruction of the tropical rain forests and the countryside, the elimination of animal species, the occurrence of disasters in nuclear power stations, the disposal of radioactive waste, the spread of nuclear weapons, the exhaustion of the earth's resources, the turning of productive land into desert -- all threaten to make life on this planet insupportable in a century's time.

There is a joke going around which says, "The only people who <u>aren't</u> depressed are the people who do not know what is going on."

Our nation has not experienced a major economic depression lately. Instead, it has protracted economic stress caused by a combination of the high cost of living with reduction in high paying jobs. Families make substantial investment in their children's education, only to discover that returns on that investment in terms of a good job are illusive. Can this generation as easily obtain the standard of living their parents had? Perhaps not.

Another factor creating the second epidemic of depression in this century relates to social upheaval. Canadian research indicates that social upheaval "results in the breakdown of social cohesion and increases social disorganization, which is reflected in increased rates of mental illness" (Klerman, 1984). Loss is a factor in social change. During times of dramatic change, social structure and traditional patterns are altered. Depression is more likely during transitions when familiar patterns are gone and a new way of life has not yet been established.

The dramatic changes since World War II have been the subject of many magazine articles and television documentaries. We feel it in every aspect of our lives: in the communications sector with the advent of satellites, in health with the development of new life-saving procedures, in politics as empires break down creating opportunities as well as instabilities. With just these few examples illustrating change, we can appreciate why stress is an important factor in recent decades.

Dr. Gold (1987), like so many others, describes our era as marked by extreme and exceedingly rapid changes.

> Throughout the world, we are in an era of social, political and technological revolution. The science we learn in school is invalid by the time we reach adulthood. The computer is second nature to our children, but to many parents and grandparents this fundamental new tool will remain a mystery. Children have power and independence unheard of just a short time ago. Teenagers murder. Teenagers commit suicide. Life expectancy is longer, but money runs out. Conquer heart disease and what do you get? Cancer. Horrible diseases like AIDS appear out of nowhere.

When I was a child, my parents were worried about polio. Now, we worry about Lyme's Disease. We may have eradicated smallpox with our vaccines, but there is no vaccine for AIDS. Over optimism that disease can be eradicated through scientific discovery has been tempered by the reality that occurs with the arrival of new diseases. And as antibiotics become less effective against more resilient strains of bacteria, old diseases once again become a problem. We are no more able to eliminate disease than we are of eliminating war. The changing realities of life may be one reason for the rise of depressive illness in the 1970's and 80's. Gold (1987, p. 190) writes, "Depression is believed to be on the rise worldwide, perhaps even epidemic."

Our shift from an Age of Anxiety (the term used to describe the era follow the dropping of the atomic bomb) to an Age of Depression (the term that could describe the era of slowly declining economic prosperity for the average wage earner, slowly rising cost of living, and accelerating demands to cope with continuous change) produces a general sense of loss. We may be living in a time when some of the changes are not viewed as purposeful or meaningful and there is little optimism for the future. We have been taught to think that change means progress, and progress is good; however, progress is a two-edged sword that cuts both ways. Adapting to fast-paced, dramatic changes has made us feel vulnerable.

No one can be absolutely certain why depression is so common in the last part of the Twentieth Century. Many theories have been suggested.

A greater gap between expectations and fulfillment than in previous generations, increased drug use and greater mobility, all have been proposed as possible reasons for the increase in the 1970's and 80's. Some even suggest that a change in biological factors is at work, but conclusive evidence for any of these theories is not yet at hand (Goode, 1990, p. 53).

While scientists try to discover the cause of history's latest rise in the incidence of depression, I would emphasize one thing to anyone coping with this problem: If you have this illness or someone you love has this condition, it is not your fault. Whether the depression is due to some general, overriding environmental factor, such as the stress of life in the last part of this century, or if the depression is more related to genetic factors, as it was for my son, or if the depression is caused by a combination of environmental factors and genetic predisposition, which is often the case, it still is not your fault. Depression is similar to many other illnesses such as cancer, heart disease, or diabetes. Like them, there seems to be genetic factors or environmental/lifestyle factors or (most commonly) a combination of both the genetic and environmental/lifestyle factors which affect the formation of the illness. For example, cigarette smoking is a lifestyle factor that can affect cancer and heart disease. Obesity resulting from overeating can also contribute to the development of those same illnesses, as well as diabetes. Yet, genetics is a strong factor in predicting who is likely to be at risk for developing cancer, heart disease, and diabetes. Genetics and lifestyle all combine to produce risk.

No one would blame the victim of cancer, heart disease, or diabetes for their conditions, nor would anyone blame their parents. The same should be said about depression. If you are depressed or your child experiences depressive illness, it is not anyone's fault that this condition exists. Once this fact is fully understood and appreciated, there will be less guilt associated with depressive illness and more willingness to seek treatment. Depression is now being recognized as a physiological problem: e.g., a problem caused by neurotransmitters and/or hormones. As we come to know the biology of this illness, it will allow us to be more objective about the condition, seeing it as a medical condition, not a sign of personal weakness.

Today's challenge for the person who has the condition, or their loved ones, is to recognize depression as a treatable medical condition. The optimistic news about depression is that the National Institute of Mental Health has done a nationwide study which has determined the existence of a number of highly effective treatments. The problem with depression lies not so much in its treatment (the success rate is at least 80 percent) but in lack of recognition or diagnosis of the condition as a treatable illness. Sometimes persons with the condition fail to seek medical help; other times they go to their doctor, telling them of their symptoms, and the physician does not diagnosis it. This means we, as the general public, need to know the symptoms of depression if we are to cope with the number one public health problem.

TYPES OF DEPRESSIVE ILLNESS

To get a fuller perspective on depression, it is helpful to include a description of the many forms it can take. I will use Ben as an example when it applies because, unfortunately for him, he exemplifies several different forms of depressive illness. I know I have his blessing in doing this, because once when I was teaching an adult evening class, I asked Ben if I could use one of his experiences as an example. His response was: "If it can be used to help someone else, go right ahead."

Dysthymia

Dysthymia is a chronic depressive condition in which people feel out of sorts all of the time. They are not deeply depressed, but neither do they feel good. Weather makes a useful analogy to describe the mood of people suffering from dysthymia. Their mood is not like a thunderstorm (dark and dangerous), but neither do they experience blue skies and sunshine. One could say their world is gray and overcast most of the time. They are generally unhappy, although they may put on a smile to allow others to feel more comfortable. Virginia Commonwealth University clinical psychologist James McCullough says, "Researchers estimate that nearly 9 million Americans are locked in dysthymia's dispiriting grip, `It's like a low-grade infection....Dysthymics never really feel good' (Goode, 1990, p. 51).

Ben had dysthymia. Depression was a fairly constant condition throughout his childhood. Ben told his psychiatrist he felt depressed all of his life. His medical records include this notation: "He states that he does not remember a time when he has felt happy most of the time."

Dysthymia is not just a minor depressive problem. A booklet published by the National Institute of Mental Health states,

> Some people with dysthymia also have episodes of major depression, their symptoms becoming dramatically more severe for a while and then returning to their usual reduced level. These people are said to have double depression, that is, dysthymia plus major depression. Individuals with double depression are at much higher risk for recurring episodes of major depression, so careful treatment and follow-up are very important (Sargent, 1989a).

SAD (Seasonal Affective Disorder)

Living in northern Minnesota, I have been especially interested in one of the newer discoveries about depression. What we always called "the winter blahs," are scientifically defined as Seasonal Affective Disorder. Researchers indicate that for people suffering from SAD "despair sets in with the disappearance of the lingering daylight hours of summer and persists for as long as short days and the cold winter sun remain. As spring returns, however, patients with SAD feel their energy return. Their desolation lifts and their lives return to normal." (Goode, 1990, p. 51).

There may be a correlation between this pattern in humans and what animals experience in winter. People with SAD, like hibernating animals, "crave sleep, they also binge on carbohydrates, gaining weight from October through March." (Gelman, 1987, p. 54). The over-eating and over-sleeping with SAD is interesting because people with other common forms of depressive conditions under-eat and lack the ability to sleep.

What causes SAD? "The culprit may be a sleep inducing hormone called melatonin, which is produced in the dark. Or, as other researchers now believe, SAD may be a biological phenomenon left over from prehistoric man, who conserved energy during the cold winter months when food was scarce." (Gelman, 1987, p. 54).

People with seasonal depression are helped by sitting close to a bank of lights that emit rays similar to natural light. Patients in the past sat 3 feet away from the light and stayed there for 2 hours. If you put the same light 15 inches away, you may only need a 30 minute treatment. Some people find the new desk-top lights convenient. One-half of people with winter depression are bipolar (manic-depression), whereas people with unipolar depression may experience changes in mood in the spring and fall when in the rate change of sun light is at it greatest.

Ben's psychiatrist told me he probably had seasonal depression. She noted his increase in symptoms during the colder months and a rise in energy as warmer weather came.

Some people with SAD move closer to the equator for part of the winter. I think of our vacations in Florida each winter and feel they may have done him more good than I realized at the time.

Reactive Depression

Reactive depressions are a reaction to an event or condition in one's life. These depressions can be severe, but most people recover without necessarily experiencing other recurrences. Often it is a loss of some kind. Grief has been interpreted as a normal form of reactive depression.

Recurring Unipolar Depression

People with recurring unipolar depressions (periods of low mood wthout obvious manic episodes) feel low with or without stressors in the environment. These people have normal moods much of the time, but have a number of depressive episodes during their lifetime. The National Institute of Mental Health describes the symptoms:

1. *persistent sadness*
2. *low energy*
3. *loss of interest in activities*
4. *feeling of hopelessness, guilt, worthlessness*
5. *difficulty with sleep, memory, concentration*
6. *chronic aches or persistent bodily symptoms*
    (Sargent,1989a).

Unipolar depression is especially important to understand simply because it is the most common form of depression.

Bipolar Illness

Victims of bipolar illness (also known as manic-depressive disorder) enjoy normal moods some of the time. When they have bouts of this illness, they alternate between depression and mania. When depressed, they experience symptoms of unipolar depression, but persons with bipolar illness also have times when they are high or manic. The National Institute of Mental Health (NIMH) says that when persons with bipolar are in a manic phase of the cycle, they typically have:

1. *increased energy*
2. *decreased need for sleep*
3. *increased risk-taking*
4. *feelings of mood elevation or irritability*
5. *aggressive response to frustration.*
   (Sargent, 1989,a, p. 20).

Bipolar illness comes in two forms. People with bipolar I have manic episodes that can be extreme. During these highs, they have an unrealistic belief in their own abilities; they may incur horrendous debts and make poor business decisions. They show an increase in talking, as well as physical and social activity. People around them see them as "hyper." There can be an increase in sexual activity to the point of promiscuity. People tend to overlook the painful or harmful consequences of their manic behavior. Their high energy and possibly aggressive response to frustration may even result in breaking the law and landing in jail. All of this may be associated with loss of friends, family, and employment. Not all people with bipolar I have all of these symptoms and most are helped with lithium. If you took chemistry in school you saw lithium on the chart of basic natural elements. Lithium has proven to be very effective in stabilizing the highs for persons with bipolar illness. Besides lithium, physicians are now using some of the medications traditionally used to control epilepsy for people with bipolar illness. Some bipolar patients are helped by carbamazapine, others are helped by valproate.

All indications were that Ben did not have Bipolar I. Ben's illness corresponds to the symptoms of Bipolar II. His highs did not get extremely high; his manic episodes would have been called hypomanic (small manic). For example, his increased talking was mildly disruptive to family conversations, but a casual observer might not have seen him as excessively talkative. His increased physical activity caused him to get too carried away during roughhouse play. Ben loved to wrestle with his dad and when he was younger his father would just hold him down when Ben got a little out of control. But during the last year, there were several times in which Ben, quite unintentionally, hurt his dad when he got carried away when they wrestled.

Our daughter, Caroline, discovered early in her childhood that playing with Ben was often difficult if not impossible, because he would get physically out of control. His hypomanic behavior meant that he was not hyper all of the time, but there were times when his behavior was excessive. He did not seem to be able to control this. He never intended to hurt anyone and was always remorseful or confused as to what had come over him.

Whenever I would read those neat lists of manic behaviors contrasted to depression, I was always a little frustrated because it seemed to me that Ben was both manic and depressed at the same time. I have since learned that 2/3 of people with bipolar illness experience mixed states. Dr. Kay Jamison writes, "Mixed states represent a critical combination of dysphoric mood (anxiety plus depression), depressed thought combined with an exceptionally perturbed, agitated and unpleasant physical state that is usually accompanied by a heightened energy level and increased impulsivity." (Lifesaver, Summer, 1994). It is interesting to note that there is a high rate of attempted suicide during mixed states.

MULTIPLICITY OF DEPRESSIVE CONDITIONS

In this short look at the various ways depression manifests itself, it is clear the term "depression" is not just one illness but a cluster of conditions. These conditions overlap, and it is possible, if not common, for one person to have a number of them rather than just one. For example, I saw Ben as having bipolar II, and his therapist was able to identify the dysthymia and seasonal depression. Scientists call Ben's combination (dysthymia plus bipolar II) cyclothymia. Dr. Gold (1987) writes that "cyclothymics come from bipolar families." Our son had a number of overlapping conditions, but what is paradoxical is that, to the casual observer, this boy with a ready smile did not seem depressed at all. He, like perhaps as many as 40 percent of children and adolescents with mild to severe depression, was not seen as having a medical condition requiring help.

The Symptoms of
Depression in the Young

W hy are we so blind to childhood depression? McKnew, Cytryn and Yahraes (1983) give us their opinion:

> Perhaps the biggest reason is that many depressed children are often the 'nicest' boys and girls on the block and the best behaved kids in school.   Go into a classroom and you'll find that the kids in the back rows are the quiet ones, the ones that don't give anyone any trouble, though we know now that many of them are depressed . . . Unless you know a depressed child quite well and are really looking for signs of depression, you probably won't notice anything wrong.

Depression in children does not always look like depression in adults.   Depression in youngsters and adults is fundamentally the same illness, but depressed young people rarely have long, sad faces.   They frequently have beautiful wide smiles, trying hard not to be a burden to others, attempting to make the best of their painful lives.   If we use only the list of adult symptoms, we will miss the vast majority of   children and adolescents suffering from depression.

Lists of symptoms of depression in youngsters have been proposed in the past. Often these lists emphasize changes in the child's behavior, but I do not always find lists that emphasize change to be helpful. For example, children with dysthymia are always feeling somewhat blue. Their depression is not a change in behavior, it is the way they feel every day of their lives. Furthermore, children such as Ben who have bipolar illness have a condition with a very early onset. These children have behaviors, body complaints, frequent illnesses, and mood problems throughout their lives. Their depression is not a change; it is the way they have always been.

Children with recurring unipolar depression, on the other hand, *do* have normal mood most of the time. A change in mood does signal the onset of a bout with depression for them. I do not want to discount the value of using a change in behavior as useful in diagnosing depression. I just wish to point out that "change" shouldn't be exclusively used as a criteria in defining depression.

This list by Dr. Carl P. Malmquist of the University of Minnesota avoids referring to change. His symptom list describing childhood depression includes:

1. *Persistent sadness, in contrast to the temporary unhappy moods that normally occur in all children from time to time.*
2. *Low self-concept.*
3. *Provocative, aggressive behavior, or other behavior that leads people to reject or avoid the child.*

4. Proneness to be disappointed easily when things do not go exactly as planned.

5. Physical complaints such as headaches, stomach aches, sleep problems or fatigue, similar to those experienced by depressed adults.

Using Ben as an example where appropriate, I will expand on these five symptoms and then list some which other experts have noted.

1. Persistent sadness, in contrast to the temporary unhappy moods that normally occur in all children from time to time.

What are the conditions that might cause persistent sadness? Children with dysthymia suffer from chronic low mood. Children who suffer from recurring unipolar depression may have the first episode of that condition when they are quite young. Children with bipolar illness have a cyclical condition. Although they will feel normal some of the time, high moods alternate with periods of feeling low. Finally, children who experience a loss of some kind may be beginning a reactive depression that warrants attention. Any child whose sadness persists over a few weeks should be considered for some sort of treatment.

2. Low Self-concept

Depressed children typically have problems with self-esteem. It is a mistake to assume their low self-esteem is always a direct result of environmental factors. Even when parents are very loving and careful to avoid criticizing the child, the depressive illness itself can produce an attitude of self-criticism and low self-esteem for the youngster.

Some depressed children have an overly-sensitive disposition which causes them to interpret any general comment as a criticism. This overly sensitive reaction also interferes with their willingness to ask for help in the classroom. This over-sensitivity results in the perception that other children are picking on them, when in fact this is not true. Ben perceived lots of bullies in the school yard that probably did not exist; playing with neighborhood children often ended with Ben crying and returning home. His over-sensitivity meant he cried easily and generally had problems getting along with peers. Again, the child's overly-sensitive nature may not have anything to do with the actions of parents who may be doing everything they can to help the child feel confident and secure.

3. Provocative, aggressive behavior, or other behavior that lead people to reject or avoid the child.

Our daughter learned early in her childhood that Ben was difficult to play with. He would provoke disputes between them. Caroline also noted that when he became aggressive he would either lash out at others or inflict self-injury, such as biting himself. She and her playmates included Ben in their play some of the time, but because they knew that excluding him would mean they could play peacefully, they frequently chose to avoid him.

Ben had marked increases in anger and aggressive behavior when he reached fourth grade. He verbalized his anger, and broke things like pens and pencils. He also did damage in the house by carving on woodwork and defacing furniture. When Ben began seeing a psychiatrist, he mentioned that "his feeling of depression had been worse since about fourth grade." The paradox of the anger expressed by someone with depression is that some of it seems legitimate. Depressed children have every right to feel angry at being misunderstood. They have a right to feel angry at being expected to do things they simply are not able to do. Ben found deep breathing and relaxation methods helpful in controlling his angry feelings.

4. *Proneness to be disappointed easily when things do not go exactly as planned.*

Ben had a very low tolerance for frustration. When putting together a puzzle, he often pounded on a piece if it did not fit. He did the same to other toys when they did not perform as he wanted. When we would go on a family outing and there was a change or delay in plans, he easily became upset. I have wondered if this proneness to express disappointment is a forerunner to hopelessness and helplessness. Persons with depression often have errors in their thinking which lead them to be more pessimistic than others.

5. *Physical complaints such as headaches, stomach aches, sleep problems, or fatigue, similar to those experienced by depressed adults.*

Physical pain is a common indicator of childhood depression. People do not generally think of bodily pain in conjunction with depression, but it can be an important symptom. Ben told me about the pains in his arms and legs, but at the time I assumed it was the beginning of childhood arthritis, a condition my husband had when he was a child. I never thought of it as a symptom of depression. Headache pain may be especially important. Ben's childhood was plagued by frequent, painful headaches. Researchers have found that persons who experience frequent migraines have a suicide rate three times higher than people who do not.

Depressed children not only have various aches and pains, but are also frequently ill. This may be due to the effect their depression is having on the immune system. As one person said, "When you are depressed, nothing works well." This includes the immune system. The frequent illness some depressed children have contributes to the aches and pains they experience.

One of the hallmarks of depression is sleep abnormalities. Trouble with sleep can either involve insomnia -- difficulty falling asleep or staying asleep; or the opposite -- sleeping too much. Some children are energized at night and then chronically tired during the day, which adds to their problem with concentration and alertness in school. Ben's difficulties with sleep showed up immediately in infancy, and he did not sleep through the night until he was in his second or third year. Problems with sleep continued throughout his life, and he reported feeling tired at school.

6. *Inability to concentrate*

To Dr. Malmquist's list of symptoms of childhood depression I would add the inability to concentrate. Depressed children have trouble with schoolwork. Psychiatrist and author, Dr. Mark Gold writes about the reciprocal connection between depression and school difficulties in a paragraph headed "Learning Disabilities = Depression, Depression = Learning Disabilities." He says,

> Psychologist David Goldstein conducted a five-year study of 159 learning-disabled children in Philadelphia and found that nearly all of them were depressed. The school problems caused the depression in most of them; but for about one-third, depression produced the school problems.

> (Gold, 1987)

Scientists have discovered that the limbic system of the brain is of great importance to a person's learning ability. They also hypothesize that depression is a problem of the limbic system. Little wonder depressed children have learning problems! They may not be able to follow what their teachers say; consequently they do not perform to their potential.

There are a number of factors that facilitate the vicious circle regarding learning problems and depression. First of all, depressed persons of any age have difficulty concentrating. Add to this a phenomena common in animals as well as in persons called "learned helplessness." Learned helplessness occurs when people or animals find themselves in highly stressful or painful situations which they can neither get out of nor manage to cope with successfully. Children with learning problems are in the classic situation which produces learned helplessness. They are forced to be in a school situation they cannot escape from or cope with successfully. It's easy to see why children with learning problems may begin to feel helpless and hopeless. Ben had both manic-depressive illness and an attention deficit disorder. Either one would have created some problems for him in school; together they served to make his experience with school impossible.

7. Energy fluctuations

The energy levels of depressed children can fluctuate from normal to hyperactivity and then to sluggishness. Parents find themselves alternating between wanting the child to settle down, and then later wishing the child would do something other than just vegetating in front of the television set. If the child is over-watching TV and not enjoying more active games or hobbies with friends, this may be a clue to some level of depression.

Energy fluctuations are especially true for children with bipolar illness. Pioneer psychiatrist in the treatment of bipolar illness and author Dr. Ronald Fieve (1975) describes bipolar children this way: "Bursts of aggressiveness and frantic activity may alternate with periods of sluggish passivity in a way that resembles the periodic fluctuations of adult moodswings." It is important to suspect bipolar illness in young children because Dr. Gold (1987) states, "many earlier-onset depressions are now believed to be bipolar II depressions."

8. Eating problems

Another hallmark of depression is eating abnormalities. The child will either eat too little, consequently becoming thin, or eat too much and carry extra weight. Although Ben ate only small quantities of formula as a newborn, he ate frequently and had normal weight. Throughout most of his life Ben struggled with overeating which is consistent with bipolar II. From his work with young patients, Dr. Charles Popper (1990) writes, "appetite and body weight may exhibit marked fluctuations in bipolar children." Dr. Gold (1987) also cites bipolar II as the type of depression with "reverse" symptoms. Patients tend to oversleep rather than have difficulty sleeping and tend to "eat and eat instead of losing their appetites." The connection between eating problems and depressive illness makes me wonder how many overweight children are suffering from an undiagnosed case of depressive illness.

9. Bladder and Bowel Problems

Bedwetting is mentioned by many psychiatrists including Drs. Gold and Fieve. It is mentioned in relationship to both anxiety and depression. Ben was toilet trained at 2 1/2, but bedwetting started at age five. Nothing we tried was successful in treating this problem. Not every child who has bedwetting episodes is depressed or anxious. But if a parent or doctor sees a cluster of symptoms indicative of either anxiety or depression in addition to the bedwetting, it is possible the wetting is part of either of them. Dr. Klerman also notes that constipation is a common experience in persons with depression. Ben had problems with this from infancy. Not only was it another physical symptom for him to contend with, but treating it was unpleasant.

10. Excessive fearfulness

Fear is one of the major symptoms of anxiety disorder. Because anxiety most often accompanies depression, it is useful to include it as a symptom commonly found in depressed young people. The world is a scary place for depressed children who also suffer from anxiety. It is filled with danger and menace. It puzzles parents to see excessive fearfulness in their child when they are providing the youngster with a safe and secure environment. This certainly was the case with our family. I thought it would be possible to teach Ben to be unafraid by being calm myself and by giving him information that demonstrated the safety of the situation. Although those strategies are generally advisable and I had some success, I was unable to calm those fears completely.

11. Impulsivity

Impulsivity -- acting without thinking about the consequences -- is a major characteristic of children with an attention deficit but is also found in some youngsters with depression. This is especially true of children with bipolar (manic-depressive) illness. Scientific evidence is mounting that bipolar depression is genetically determined. Dr. Gold (1987, p.286) reports, "Many investigators now believe that children who begin a depressed course before puberty are probably genetically driven into such an early expression of the illness." Impulsive children may have either bipolar illness, an attention deficit, or both. Some experts believe there are many more depressed children with this diagnosis than it was previously thought.

A Perspective on Childhood Depression

Two provocative quotes from Dr. Gold give both a perspective on depressive illness and a feeling for how children with the condition are often misunderstood.

He writes, "Depression in adults and children is remarkably alike...While the symptoms too are similar -- sleep and appetite disturbance, bodily complaints, hopelessness, guilt, lack of self-esteem, loss of ability to experience pleasure, fatigue and so on -- kids do not express them the same as grown-ups." As to the current lack of understanding and treatment of childhood depression, Gold (1987) states, "Many kids end up being treated for hyperactivity and learning disabilities, punished for laziness, or even placed in detention for aggressive, destructive behaviors, when depression is the primary problem."

ADOLESCENT DEPRESSION

Much of what was described as characteristic of childhood depression is also true of adolescent depression. Similarly, much of what is characteristic of adolescent depression is also applicable to childhood depression. The major difference is that often the more socially withdrawn child will become outgoing during the teen years, only to once again return to being withdrawn in adulthood. This brief section on adolescent depression describes issues especially troublesome in the teen years.

Anxiety and Alcohol/Drug Use

The chapter, "Anxiety and Suicide Prevention," gives extensive information on the role that high anxiety states play in increasing the risk of suicide for people with depression. It also addresses the dangers of using alcohol and/or drugs to self-treat anxiety. Parents, teachers and health professionals need to be aware that adolescents who are depressed and anxious frequently self-medicate their condition by using alcohol and/or street drugs.

Hormones

Another factor frequently found in adolescence is the interplay of hormones and depression. The blossoming of sexuality and the connection between hormone balances and mood makes the adolescent especially susceptible to depression. It is not within the scope of this book to fully describe the connection between how brain chemistry can affect hormones and, conversely, how hormones in other parts of the body can affect depressive symptoms. One just needs to look at the high rate of suicide attempts, especially by teenage girls, to get an appreciation for the interplay of changing hormone levels and depression. Or just think about what we are now learning about PMS (pre-menstrual syndrome). These emotional storms of adolescence are especially difficult for young persons suffering from dysthymia who are already battling low mood.

The role of hormones in depression is just beginning to be understood as playing a part in a wider picture of chemical imbalance. This quote from a recent publication summarizes how far we have come in recognizing the bigger picture:

"In the early days of research, scientists thought in terms of relatively simple models of chemical imbalance. Depression, for example, was thought to stem from an insufficiency of norepinephrine, one of many substances mediating the transmission of nerve impulses in the brain. Now, few experts talk about 'too much' or 'too little' of a single chemical. Instead, they believe mood disorders are the result of a complex interplay among a variety of chemicals, including neurotransmitters and hormones." (Goode, 1990, p. 55).

Disappointments in Love

Adolescence is also when kids fall in love for the first time. This makes them vulnerable to reactive depression, the mood disorder caused by a loss of some kind. I have frequently heard parents of a young person who committed suicide preface their description of what happened with the remark, "He had broken up with his girlfriend," or "She had broken up with her boyfriend."

Personality Factors

Psychiatrists have observed a number of personality characteristics that makes one especially vulnerable to depression. Dr. Gold (1987) writes, "Persons who are worriers and perfectionists are known to be vulnerable to depression. Extraordinarily dependent individuals as well as introverts are also at risk." Dr. Klerman's (1984) research on depressed persons conducted after their recovery from a depressive episode also gives a profile of the personality factors which make people especially vulnerable to mood disorders.   He writes, "The depressed patient who emerges in this profile is introverted, lacking in self-confidence, unassertive, dependent, pessimistic, and self-perceived as inadequate." The teen years are notorious for causing one to be hypercritical. If the adolescent's personality has a number of those other characteristics in it already, he or she is vulnerable to a depressive episode.

A GOAL

The symptoms of depression in childhood and adolescence are not so mysterious once we see them as similar to, but not exactly like, those of adults. Once parents, teachers and health care professionals truly recognize depression as a biological condition rather than someone's fault, we can begin to tackle it as we would any other health problem.

One of the most exciting prospects in the treatment of bipolar illness (a highly biological condition) is early intervention with young people. Youngsters whose parents have the condition are at high risk of becoming bipolar themselves. There may be a way of helping them during some of the vulnerable years, age 10 - 25, the age of onset of the illness for young persons today.

Researchers have discovered that once people have a manic-depressive episode, they are more likely to have future episodes. Doctors use the term "kindling" to describe the tendency for further episodes to occur more readily even without the presence of any stress in the environment. Without some form of intervention, the average number of episodes people with bipolar illness are likely to experience is sixteen.

Stability, on the other hand, tends to beget more stability. To maintain the desired stability, early administration of lithium and either carbamazapine or depakote is used during childhood, adolescence and early adulthood. Lithium has a long history of producing stability. The seizure medications block kindling. Administration of these medicines may either prevent the occurrence of the illness, or reduce the number of episodes. Even if it fails to prevent the illness from occurring, the use of these medications by young persons with a high risk for bipolar illness may serve to protect them during those years. With the suicide rate for 15 - 19 year olds throughout the early 1990's at 18/100,000 for boys and bipolar patients at high risk for suicide, I personally welcome this type of preventive medicine.

The goal is to provide the most effective, least expensive treatment to the great number of young people who suffer. By treating the young we can provide a life-long benefit to them and their families. The next chapter describes what can be done.

What's To Be Done?

The exciting news about depression is that most people can be helped. Two types of short term psychotherapies have <u>proven</u> to be effective. Sometimes these therapies can lift a depression without the use of medication, but the general consensus is that medication plus therapy gives the quickest and the best results for adults. Persons with genetically-based depression often need medication to treat their condition because it is caused by brain chemistry. The combination of chemical intervention and a psychotherapy which focuses on the behavioral manifestations of their illnesses works for at least 80% of adults suffering from depression.

Although moods do often lift on their own without the use of some type of intervention, it frequently takes six to nine months or sometimes as long as two years for the depression to lift. Medications, on the other hand, often work in a matter of weeks. Depression causes a lot of pain and can disrupt or destroy a life. Antidepressant medication is an effective, humane treatment which reduces unnecessary suffering. Some adults prefer not to use medication. Adult clients and their doctors need to work together to decide if they can work safely on the depression without the use of medication.

What about the use of prescription medications for adolescents with depression? Medications are important for some teens, and for those who benefit from them, they are a blessing.

For some they can even be life-saving. Medications, like everything else, must be approached with caution. In a recent lecture by adolescent psychology specialist Dr. Harry Hoberman, he noted that although antidepressants have proven to be effective for adults and for children, the efficacy for adolescents is not clear. This does not mean there are no teens who benefit from antidepressants; it simply means there should be a judicious use of these medications for that age group.

Just exactly why antidepressants may not have the same record of success for adolescents is not yet known. It makes me wonder if this phenomena may not relate to how body chemistry interacts with brain chemistry. In the preceding chapter, the fact that brain chemistry can produce pain in various parts of the body was explained. Later, under the subheading "hormones," it was pointed out that the converse is also true; chemicals in the body can produce symptoms of depressed mood. I do not know how the interaction of body chemistry on brain chemistry affects boys and men, but these facts about females may be relevant to the role of hormones and depression and may be a clue as to why antidepressants may not work as well for adolescents. We know that:

1. *The incidence of depression is twice as high for women as for men.*

2. *The rate of attempted suicides for adolescent females is much higher than it is for males. There are approximately 40 - 50 attempts for every completed suicide for adolescent females.*

3. *Approximately 80 percent of women experience at least a mild case of post-partum depression.*

4. *The phenomena of pre-menstrual syndrome involves many of the symptoms of depression.*

5. *Girls typically out-perform boys academically until the beginning of adolescence. Since there is a connection between depression and decreased ability to concentrate, hormonal changes that affect mood may be part of the cause of declined school performance.*

Hormonal changes in adolescents may become identified as one of the reasons antidepressants have not yet been proven to show the same level of efficacy for teenagers as they have for children or adults.

It is also interesting to note that the course of life-long depressive illness in high level primates (monkeys and apes) is similar to that of humans. Scientists have observed these animals in their natural habitat and found that depressed young primates are socially withdrawn during childhood, more socially outgoing as adolescents and then return to withdrawal during adulthood. Can these findings give hints to the biological reasons why antidepressant may not have the same efficacy for adolescents as they do for children and adults?

With this question in mind, it becomes evident that non-medication techniques that have proven helpful for people with depression need to be the key component in a program to help depressed young people. The National Institute of Mental Health sponsored a collaborative study on the treatment of depression. They studied the effectiveness of two different psychotherapies: cognitive therapy and interpersonal therapy. Both were found to be effective for mood disorders. Cognitive therapy focuses on the thinking errors made by the depressed people. During therapy, patients develop an awareness of the illogical nature of some of their assumptions, are guided to formulate more logical statements about the circumstances in their lives, and are taught to apply reasonable solutions to their problems. Cognitive therapy does not dwell on what happened to them in the past; it focuses on the here and now. Cognitive therapy is compatible with a classroom setting because the clients' work involves writing and homework.

The second effective treatment for depression focuses on the problems the patient is currently having with interpersonal relationships. The work involves developing social competency with people in their lives right now, such as spouses, friends, family members, colleagues, neighbors, and other social contacts.

One of the most cost-effective methods of helping young people with mild to severe depression is to offer a psychology class which teaches the basics of cognitive and interpersonal therapy. Cognitive therapy teaches logic as it applies to one's personal life. Interpersonal therapy teaches social competency. A class focusing on, personal logic and interpersonal skills would easily fit into the curriculum of a psychology class. This class would be useful to anyone with a mild to severe case of depression, as well as anyone interested in personal growth. The class could be offered as a social studies elective in any junior high, senior high, college, or technical school. Since depression affects the ability of a student to concentrate, a class such as this has the potential to generally assist the student academically. It more than justifies its existence as an important element in the academic curriculum of any school.

To understand what would be taught in a class like this, and to comprehend the ways depression manifests itself in illogical thinking and social problems, a description of these therapies is helpful. As the thinking errors found in depression are described, you will come to see just how common mild forms of depression are in our society today, and how the huge population of young people with mild cases of depression would benefit from a class in personal logic and interpersonal skills.

COGNITIVE THERAPY

Depressed people do not perceive what is happening in their environment accurately, and they do not think logically. One could say their thinking is distorted. Depressed individuals are not crazy; they just are not as logical as they could be. For example, hopelessness and helplessness result from the lack of clear perception of a life situation. Illogical conclusions are made and few options seem apparent. Cognitive therapy's focus on thinking errors is a straight-forward psychotherapy for depression, since it works directly with the problems people have. It teaches people to think more logically; in other words, to think straight.

Cognitive therapy was pioneered by Dr. Aaron Beck. It deals with pervasive negativity of thought patterns, identifies gross distortions in a patient's thinking, and allows people to be more objective and realistic. Dr. Beck identified ten common thinking errors depressed persons make. A colleague, Dr. David Burns (1980), describes these in his book Feeling Good. A brief summary of these common distortions in personal logic gives a picture of depressed thinking.

1. All-or-Nothing Thinking

This describes thinking of yourself in black-or-white terms. Depressed people think they are supposed to be absolutely perfect at all times. We are human, less than perfect. Depression causes self-critical thinking. Any mistake or any imperfection causes depressed persons to think they are a complete loser. This illogical perfectionism is the reason straight-A students feel like a failure just for getting one B on a test. When you expect to be perfect at all times, you fear any kind of mistake. The exaggerated expectation of all-or-nothing thinking sets people up for impossible demands and feelings of inadequacy and worthlessness for just being human.

2. Overgeneralization

Overgeneralization causes depressed people to think that something negative that happened in the past will happen again and again. The emotional pain depressed people feel from rejection is often caused by overgeneralization. An assumption is made that since one person rejected you, all people will respond in exactly the same way. There is no evidence for this assumption and it is illogical, but when depressed persons overgeneralize, they think that since there was one negative experience, there will always be negative reactions from people.

3. Mental Filter

This refers to the tendency to focus on a negative detail of a situation and then dwell on it. Exclusively focusing on a negative detail causes depressed people to think the whole situation is bad. Dr. Burns writes that it is as if depressed people are wearing a pair of eyeglasses that filters out all the good things in life and allows only the negative to be viewed. They do not know that what they see is distorted. They only know that what they perceive consists totally of negative experiences.

4. Disqualifying the Positive

Even more tragic is the distortion of translating a totally neutral or even potentially good experience into something negative. Depressed people with this thinking error do not ignore positive experiences; they distort them. An appreciation for this cognitive problem gives insight into why people will feel so badly even when wonderful things are happening to them. In the midst of outer circumstances that are positive, the lives of depressed people become a nightmare where everything is awful. They think of themselves as losers, worthless pieces of humanity. If the depression is less severe, disqualifying the positive may take the form of thinking of themselves as second-rate. This error in logic and perception is probably one of the most destructive distortions, because people maintain negative beliefs about themselves in the face of objective evidence to the contrary.

5. Jumping to Conclusions

Rather than being logical, depressed persons leap to conclusions that are not warranted by evidence. Dr. Burns gives two examples of this:

> **Mind reading**: Depressed people assume others have the same low opinion of them that they have of themselves. Convinced of their own worthlessness,. they never confirm this conclusion with facts. The scientific method of checking an hypothesis (to discover the truth) would help to correct this error in logic.

> **The Fortune Teller Error**: As they think of the future, depressed people jump to the conclusion that something terrible is going to happen. Predictions of coming disaster fit into their thinking even when they are unrealistic.

6. Magnification and Minimization

With magnification, any small error or challenge can become an overwhelmingly difficult problem. This distortion has sometimes been called catastrophizing because it can transform a fairly typical negative situation into a catastrophe. With minimization, any strength, any talent, or any good fortune is seen as something very small and insignificant. Depressed people combine these two distortions by magnifying their imperfections and minimizing their assets, a process that will always create a perception of being at best second rate and at worst a complete loser.

7. Emotional Reasoning

If people use their emotions as proof of their assumptions, the conclusion depressed people draw will be negative. One of the examples Dr. Burns gave of this form of logic was 'I feel like a dud, therefore I am a dud.' Moods reflect what we think and what we believe. If our thinking is distorted, our moods are distorted. Taking the negative moods as proof that we are bad or useless has no basis. Many depressed persons feel very guilty. Using emotional reasoning, they use the negative emotion of guilt as their proof that they must have done something bad. Other examples Dr. Burns cited are feelings of being overwhelmed as proof their problems are impossible resolve, feelings of inadequacy as proof they are worthless, low mood as proof they should do nothing. A secondary effect of this form of distortion is procrastination.

8. "Should" Statements

Depression can cause low energy. Depressed people may try to get themselves going by using "should" statements like, 'I should do this' or 'I should do that.' Any statement that tries to force or shame them into doing something causes an artificial pressure and creates resentment. Instead of motivating them to do something, it has the opposite effect by making them feel apathetic. These statements turn up the emotional stress. Setting a standard for themselves with statements of what they must or should do and then falling short of this artificial standard adds to their self-loathing.

9. Labeling and Mislabeling

This refers to the process by which they create a totally negative self-concept that is based on thinking errors.   It is overgeneralization in its extreme form. Labeling themselves as a loser, as worthless, as a hopeless case is both simplistic and inaccurate. It is done from feelings of inadequacy, rather than from genuine insight.

10. Personalization

This distortion causes people to take responsibility for something when there is no basis in fact for them to do so. Depressed people draw the conclusion that what happened was their fault or in some way is a reflection of their inadequacy. Personalization causes unnecessary, uncalled-for guilt.   Their sense of guilt is burdensome to the point of being crippling. Feeling that what others do is their responsibility means the weight of the world is on their shoulders.

Implications and Application of Cognitive Therapy

These ten cognitive errors or distortions are common in our time. If these thinking patterns are familiar to you, you can now see why some scientists believe depression to be epidemic during the 1970's, 80's and 90's. If you feel overwhelmed just reading the list, you understand how depressed people feel.

Dr. Beck's therapy helps patients take an aggressive approach with their illogical thoughts. He emphasizes self help by outlining a three-step program to help patients deal with these distortions. Patients actively work during the session and do homework during the eight to twelve weeks of therapy. The three-step system consists of:

1. *Training themselves to both recognize and record in writing the self-critical thoughts as they occur.*

2. *Labeling these thoughts as distortions.*

3. *Talking back to these distortions by presenting a more realistic self-evaluation of the situation. (Burns, 1980)*

In addition to the work in changing thinking patterns, Beck's cognitive therapy works to change depressed people's pattern of doing nothing -- a result of their feeling helpless. Taking positive action can make a substantial change in the way they feel. Cognitive therapy is a multifaceted approach with proven results. It is a non-medication program which not only reduces the pain of a depressive episode but often helps to prevent future occurrences of the condition. It has great potential of helping groups of adolescents and young adults deal with mild to severe cases of depression.

INTERPERSONAL THERAPY (IPT)

Cognitive therapy is not the only short term, focused psychotherapy with proven efficacy. The other is the interpersonal therapy described by Dr. Gerald Klerman. It is designed specifically for the treatment of depression, and like cognitive therapy, it was investigated as part of the large scale, multi-site research project known as the NIMH Collaborative Study of Psychotherapy of Depression. IPT's effectiveness is well established. Like cognitive therapy, IPT focuses on some of the specific symptoms of depression.

An analysis of the list of symptoms of mood disorders reveals a cluster of issues revolving around the problems people have getting along with others. Children, adolescents, and adults with depression often are angry and irritable, dependent, fearful, unable to experience pleasure, socially isolated, or withdrawn. They suffer from low self-esteem and low energy. Depressed people with those symptoms may not be anyone's first choice for a friend. The interpersonal aspects of depression consequently are as fruitful an avenue for work as are the cognitive distortions.

The basic premise of Dr. Klerman's IPT is that depression occurs within an interpersonal context. He believes that intervention and training which focus on the interpersonal context helps people recover from a mild or severe depression and may even help to prevent future depression. Klerman's focused, short-term program emphasizes the patient's specific problems with current interpersonal relations. Although there is full recognition of the importance genetics and brain chemistry have in predisposing the individual to depression and an understanding that personal history and personality factors also play an important role in causing vulnerability to depression, IPT focuses on how to deal with the social problems resulting from the depressive condition. There is no in-depth analysis of the past or any attempt to change basic personality. IPT focuses instead on "current disputes, frustrations, anxieties, and wishes as defined in the interpersonal context." (Klerman, 1984, p. 7).

Dr. Klerman's approach relies on well-established techniques such as:

1. *reassurance,*
2. *clarification of emotional states,*
3. *improvement of interpersonal communication,*
4. *testing of perceptions and performance through interpersonal contact.*

IPT is a no-fault approach to teaching social skills. The fact that young people with depression lack interpersonal skills is not their fault. The significant people in their lives (their parents, teachers, friends) may not be at fault either. Past and current interpersonal problems are related to the depression, but they are not necessarily anyone's fault. Klerman reminds us that persons with serious depression may:

> Exaggerate and distort problems in their interpersonal relations because of their current affective state and cognitive dysfunction. The symptoms of the depression.... and the patient's personality may make the people less competent to establish mutually satisfying interpersonal relationships and maintain attachments. (Klerman, 1984)

A no-fault approach to teaching social skills is not only therapeutic, it also fits the facts. For example, any blame affixed to parents for creating the depression in a young person with a genetically driven illness like bipolar or unipolar recurrent depression cannot be supported by current research findings that do not associate the depression with low maternal care or overprotection. (Klerman, 1984). Nor is it the teacher's fault either that some students' low energy, low self-esteem, and feelings of helplessness and hopelessness may lead them to disinterest in school work. It is not the peers' fault that the anger and irritability symptoms of some types of depression makes some classmates difficult to get along with. Mostly, it is not depressed people's fault they have these symptoms. IPT, through its work with reassurance,   clarification of emotional state, improvement in communications, and testing of perceptions and performance through interpersonal contact, improves social skills and relieves depression.   It has a rightful place in the curriculum of a psychology class which can be made available in our schools.

COGNITIVE THERAPY AND IPT: A USEFUL CLASS FOR HELPING TODAY'S PROBLEMS

When describing the use of cognitive and IPT techniques (and in select cases, antidepressant medication) for the almost 40% of our population who are mildly to severely depressed, an analogy with orthodontia is useful. Many people are blessed with reasonably straight teeth and do not need braces. However, quite a sizable portion of the population do have crooked teeth. Good old Mother Nature gave them a problematic bite. It is not their fault their teeth are crooked. The teeth are not crooked because they were too weak-willed to have them come in straight. No amount of determination on their part is going to make those teeth straighten up. The same is true for people with depression. Many lucky people never experience the pain of depression, but quite a sizable portion of our population do. Through no fault of their own, they too need outside assistance.

If a person with a troublesome bite wants to go through life with straight teeth, he will have to do something about it. Sometimes an oral surgeon needs to pull out teeth to make room in the mouth before efforts are made to straighten the remaining teeth. Some people do not need to have teeth pulled; braces alone will work, but for a sizable percentage of the people needing orthodontia, teeth have to come out if the braces are going to be successful. The same is true for depression. For many adults with depression, medication is the first step in getting the help they need. Only after three to six weeks on medication will cognitive and IPT therapy be fruitful.

When orthodontists put on braces, they put pressure on those teeth to move them into a different pattern. Similarly, the cognitive therapist and the client work aggressively on illogical thoughts and overly critical perceptions. They take them in hand, getting tough with distorted logic to straighten up. This type of therapy allows people to be more objective and positive in their thinking, and ultimately begin to treat themselves more kindly. They are tough on their thinking, but good to themselves.

Once the braces are off, people often wear a retainer to keep those beautifully straightened teeth in line, so problems will not recur. Likewise, some continuing but less intense work on cognitive training can be done by the patients themselves or in support groups to retain the benefits of the new thinking patterns.

Just because you may come from a family in which there is a genetic predisposition to having a crowded bite, it does not mean you necessarily have to go through life with an unattractive smile or dental problems. Something can be done about it. It may cost some money and take some time, but the odds are you will have a very satisfactory result. The same is generally true for depressive illness. You may come from a family with a genetic predisposition to depressive illness, but there is something that you can do about it. It may cost some money and take some time, but the odds are you will have satisfactory results.

Orthodontia can be done at any age. People in their 30's, 40's and 50's can and do wear braces. But generally, braces are worn by people in their teens and twenties. We believe the problem might as well be dealt with when it first becomes apparent. Resolving the problem when the person is young gives a lifetime worth of benefit from the braces. Furthermore, since crowded teeth are harder to care for, people with a problematic bite can develop a mouthful of cavities as well.

The same is true of depression. Although some people have their first depressive episode in their 30's, 40's, 50's or beyond, today we are seeing first depressive episodes in children, teens, and people in their twenties. Parents, teachers, and doctors who recognize the symptoms of depression will want to deal with it when it first becomes apparent so that individual can have a lifetime worth of benefit from effective treatment. Furthermore, like the mouth full of cavities that people may develop, the individual with depressive illness may develop additional problems like alcohol and/or drug abuse, impaired personal relationships, problems with work, etc., that might have been avoided if they had gotten treatment when the symptoms first appeared.

I hope to see the day when the practice of mental health becomes similar to the practices of dentistry. In order for that to happen, the general public has the right to demand evidence that the money spent on helping themselves or their family members will be well spent. We all have the right to expect that the methods used have proven efficacy. If schools include an elective class using cognitive therapy and IPT, they will be using methods with proven effectiveness. It is a cost-effective means of helping the nearly 40% of our school population with mild to severe depression gain the skills they need. It will give them a lifetime of benefit.

There is one important distinction between having crooked teeth and having a genetically driven depression like bipolar and unipolar recurrent depression. Having crooked teeth will not kill you. Depression might.

Anxiety and Suicide Prevention

I f we hope to help young people at risk for committing suicide, we need to not only understand depression, but anxiety. Anxiety is a very different problem. Symptoms of anxiety can foretell who is at imminent risk for making a serious attempt or actually completing suicide.

What is anxiety? It is fearfulness in the absence of an environmental reason for fear. For example, if a child is called into the principal's office he is likely to perceive a problem and will have a reason to feel frightened. If, on the other hand, a child with average or above average academic skills feels frightened every time he enters the classroom, that is anxiety.

The symptoms of general anxiety disorder are:

A. Excessive anxiety and worry (apprehensive expectation), occurring more days than not for at least 6 months, about a number of events or activities (such as work or school performance).

B. The person finds it difficult to control the worry.

C. The anxiety and worry are associated with three (or more) of the following six symptoms (with at least some symptoms present for more days than not for the past 6 months). **Note**: Only one item is required in children.

1. *restlessness or feeling keyed up or on edge*
2. *being easily fatigued*
3. *difficulty concentrating or mind going blank*
4. *irritability*
5. *muscle tension*
6. *sleep disturbance (difficulty falling or staying asleep, or restless unsatisfying sleep (DSM-IV)*

Persons with high anxiety are prone to panic attacks. The prevalence of panic attacks was researched by Dr. Myrna Weissman (1991) as part of the Epidemiologic Catchment Area Study funded by the National Institute of Mental Health. About four percent of persons interviewed by Weissman's study had experienced such attacks. During an attack, the person had the symptoms of high anxiety, as well as experiencing: dizziness, hot and cold flashes, fainting, trembling, and a fear of dying or going crazy. As compared to the chronic state of anxiety the person usually feels, a panic attack is an acute, time-limited state of intense anxiety which produces a feel of impending doom.

Panic attacks are recurring episodes that come upon the person suddenly and unpredictably. These attacks of fear can be crippling. Persons with anxiety disorder sometimes are frightened to be alone. Not knowing when the next crippling attack might occur, panic sufferers often want the support of someone near at hand. It is also common for persons with anxiety disorder to fear public places away from home because after several attacks, they will avoid places that resemble those where episodes of panic occurred in the past. In extreme cases, the fear of having another attack will cause them to become immobile. Dr. Weissman reports that approximately 1.5% of the population have panic attacks some time in their lives that are severe or prolonged enough to be diagnosed as Panic Disorder.

Anxiety disorders are common for people with depressive illness. The term dysphoria means the combination of depression and anxiety so often seen by psychiatrists. Dr. Gerald Klerman (1984, p. 31) observed that "approximately 60 to 70 percent of depressed patients report anxiety." This was true for my son Ben. As a child he was frightened in situations in which there were no environmental reasons to feel fear. He was uncomfortable being alone or sleeping alone. We tried to encourage him to be more independent, but many nights it was kinder to allow him to fall asleep in our bed and then move him to his own once he was asleep. A picture of Ben when he was eighteen months old showed him biting his nails. This photo is helpful to me in appreciating the long-term nature of his experience with the symptoms of his anxiety disorder and the biological nature of the condition.

When he became school aged, he went to school each day, but it was not a comfortable situation for him. Unlike most young boys who are out playing with friends, Ben chose to be at home with us or with a very few other people who allowed him to feel less anxious. If he went away from home to play, he always wanted either my husband or me to go with him.

Another anxiety symptom Ben experienced was dizziness. There were times when Ben fell while walking down a short flight of stairs. He would explain that he fell because he was dizzy. His dizziness did not make any sense to me at the time, but it is indicative of his anxiety disorder.

The summer following Ben's sixth grade, I observed what I now know was a panic attack. On a camping trip Ben told me his heart was beating fast and he was frightened. His heart would not slow down, and he said he felt like he was having a heart attack. I had him lie down and do some deep breathing to help him relax until it passed. I do not recall how long the attack lasted. He rested for some time and later reported the palpitations stopped. It was a very painful experience for him to have and for me to watch. It seems a shame that a child this young should have to experience something so frightening.

Although many people have an anxiety disorder which accompanies their depressive condition, anxiety can occur alone. Suicide attempts are made by persons who experience panic attacks without the concurrent depression. Dr. Weissman (1991) discovered that "the lifetime rate of suicide attempts in persons with uncomplicated Panic Disorder (without any other problem such as depression) was seven percent, consistently higher than the one percent rate for persons with no psychiatric disorder." What is more, Dr. Weissman's research unexpectedly discovered that for all panic patients (those with anxiety disorders occurring along with other problems such as depression, as well as those with anxiety alone), the rate of suicide attempts rose to 20 percent. She writes, "Therefore, we concluded that suicide attempts were associated with Panic Disorder in its uncomplicated, or its comorbid form, and the risks were comparable to those of major depression, both comorbid and uncomplicated." These findings were substantiated by similar findings both in Europe and in Canada. They underscore the importance of treating panic attacks as one way of reducing the risk of suicide attempts.

Furthermore, clinicians want to know which of their patients are acutely suicidal and which patients have symptoms that indicate a chronic state of high suicide risk. Eminent psychiatrist Dr. Jan Fawcett analyzed the symptoms "which would discriminate highly suicidal patients from the majority of depressed patients who do not kill themselves." His preliminary findings indicate the important role anxiety plays as a risk factor.

As part of the Collaborative Program on the Psychobiology of Depression, Fawcett (1992) analyzed the one year follow-up data of 954 patients with severe depression. He found six variables "are significantly related to suicide within one year of entry into the study." These variables are:

1. *panic attack*
2. *severe psychic anxiety*
3. *diminished concentration*
4. *global insomnia*
5. *moderate alcohol abuse*
6. *severe loss of interest or pleasure (anhedonia).*

Variables that are reliable long-term predictors of suicide occurring sometime in the patients' future are:

1. *hopelessness*
2. *suicidal ideation*
3. *previous suicidal attempts. (Fawcett, 1992, p. 104)*

The importance of paying serious attention to the role high anxiety states can have on suicide attempts or completion was discussed in an interview Dr. Fawcett gave for the newsletter "Livesaver," published by the American Suicide Foundation (1991, Summer). When asked why panic attacks can prove to be deadly, his response was, "When panic attacks occur together with the hopelessness that can accompany depression, patients may begin to feel that only suicide can provide some relief. It is easy to see how someone in that situation could feel desperate and hopeless, anticipating the pain of severe panic attacks that will continue to recur." Fawcett went on to recommend educating people about the existence of Panic Disorder as a treatable condition.

The co-existence of panic attacks in persons with depression increases the risk of suicide. This is evident from the fact that "in the study's first year 62 percent of the patients who killed themselves had panic attacks together with major depression." ("Understanding," 1991). Panic attacks usually occur in about 25 to 30 percent of clients who have a serious depressive illness. Anxiety is probably the most dangerous problem a person with depression can have.

What are the implications of these findings for physicians? Dr. Fawcett says, "Patients with a major affective disorder who have marked anxiety, panic attacks or agitation, should be recognized as imminent suicide risks by the treating clinicians." These patients need to be treated pharmacologically and with other appropriate measures.

The implication of the work of Drs. Weissmann and Fawcett leads to a conclusion that clients with high anxiety levels have a high risk for attempting suicide sometime in their lives; moreover, the presence of panic attacks in depressed persons places them at imminent risk of making suicide attempts.

NON-MEDICATION TREATMENT FOR ANXIETY WITH OR WITHOUT DEPRESSION

What about the many young people whose anxiety interferes with effective functioning? Medication is often a necessary part of treatment for anxiety disorder, especially when it is severe or prolonged enough to meet the criteria for Panic Disorder and/or if the patient is seriously depressed.

There may be two type of anxiety disorders. In the first type, much that can be said about depression is also true of that type of anxiety, and it responds to the same medication -- antidepressants. The other type of anxiety disorder does not respond to antidepressants. What are the other treatments for anxiety besides medications? Are there any inexpensive means of helping young people to manage their anxiety?

In the previous chapter I suggested the development of a course that could be offered to any adolescent. It treated the major symptoms of depression: the cognitive errors and problems with interpersonal relationships. The curriculum of this class should also include elements that help young people manage their anxiety. It could include the following five items.

1. Information on the biological nature of anxiety.

Anxiety, like depression, is probably a result of biological predispositions. Anxiety disorders, like many other conditions, tend to run in families. Persons who have "a close relative with the condition were more likely to develop it than those who did not." (Sheehan, 1983). Studies suggest that "proneness to this disorder fit closely, though not perfectly, with a dominant-gene inheritance pattern." (Sheehan, 1983, p. 82). In this type of pattern, a person could inherit the disorder from just one parent.

The biological nature of the condition is also reflected in its strong association with a heart condition called mitral valve prolapse.

Among patients with panic attacks, approximately one in every three also has this disorder, which involves a floppy mitral valve in the heart. This floppy mitral valve is believed to be inherited through a dominant gene. The disorder is not usually considered a serious heart problem. Although no one yet fully understands the relationship between the two conditions, the frequent coexistence of the anxiety disease with the inherited mitral valve prolapse lends some further support to the idea that there is some genetic vulnerability to the anxiety disease. (Sheehan, 1983, pp. 82-83)

Studying characteristics of twins lends further credence to the genetic inheritability of anxiety disease. Twin studies are used to separate behavior resulting from the effects of environment versus behavior due to the effects of heredity. When identical twins are compared with non-identical twins in regard to anxiety disorders, heredity appears to be of greater importance than environment. The scientific community is now trying to discover the exact biochemical or metabolic abnormality that causes this condition.

The best guesses so far involve certain nerve endings and receptors in the central nervous system which produce and receive chemical messengers that stimulate and excite the stimulants called catecholamines. It is believed that in the anxiety disease, the nerve endings are overfiring. They are working too hard, overproducing these stimulants and perhaps others.

At the same time there are nerve endings and receptors that have the opposite effect: they produce naturally-occurring tranquilizers, called inhibitory neurotransmitters, that inhibit, calm down, and dampen the nerved firing of the brain.   It appears that the neurotransmitters or the receptors may be deficient, either in quality or quantity. (Sheehan, 1983, pp. 83-84)

Learning these facts and others relative to the biological nature of this condition is cognitively therapeutic. Persons with any illness need some reassurance that their problems are not their fault. People with anxiety disorders especially need to know their condition is a treatable medical illness. It is not a hopeless condition and they are not helpless because it exists. Like any other medical problem, it must be managed by the person who has it. Developing self-help skills is a must.

2. Teaching Breathing Techniques

Several symptoms of high anxiety states and panic attacks involve breathing: e.g., difficulty in getting breath or overbreathing, smothering or choking sensations or lump in throat, dizziness, and fainting. If we are to help people with anxiety, we must help them feel that they have more control over their breathing. When recommending a technique, I always feel more confident turning to an ancient method -- one that has withstood the test of time. Here is what eminent teacher and author Joseph Campbell (1990) says about Kundalini yoga:

> "The notion is that emotion and feeling and state of the mind are related to breath. When you are at rest, the breathing is in a nice, even order. When you are stirred with shock the breathing changes. With passion the breathing changes. Change the breathing and you change the state."

Routinely practicing yoga could be a means of decreasing part of the symptoms associated with high anxiety states. This book cannot go into great detail about yoga techniques, but Campbell gives this simple summary of how yoga is practiced. One starts with controlling the breath by means of specific breathing paces. "You breathe in through one nostril, hold, breathe out through the other nostril, hold in through the second, hold, out through the first and so forth and so on." (Campbell, 1990, p. 136).

Picture in your mind a person doing yoga, and then a person experiencing a high anxiety state. Aren't those incompatible images? Wouldn't it be advisable to use this well-established practice to help people with anxiety disorder? Yoga may provide to be a method of breath training that would reduce one of the major symptoms of high anxiety states.

3. Teaching the Use of Visualization

Visualization is useful in both raising self concept and in decreasing anxiety. The book Self-Esteem, by Matthew McKay and Patrick Fanning, describes the technique and how it works. Visualization work starts first with teaching the person to relax, to clear the mind of distractions, and to imagine positive peaceful scenes. In this calm state, students imagine themselves doing things successfully, such as interacting pleasantly with others or achieving goals easily, etc.

Visualization works to reduce the fear component of anxiety. As stated earlier, anxiety is defined as fearfulness in the absence of any environmental reasons for feeling frightened. This is how visualization works: In the relaxation phase, the instructor guides students through a process that allows them to relax every part of their body. Once relaxed, they are instructed to calmly focus on improving their ability to experience each of their senses. Students visualize a vivid scene: details of what the scene looks like, the sounds they might hear, the tactile experience they will have, what might be tasted or eaten in the place, and the smell they would encounter. As students practice forming these sensory images, they become better at doing visualization.

Once they have improved their ability to visualize, students may want to identify situations that frighten them or identify desired goals in everyday life that are blocked by anxiety states. Using visualization techniques allows them to imagine scenes in which they are calm and able to perform in a relaxed, confident manner. They imagine themselves doing what they want to do easily. Students are encouraged to practice visualization techniques at home, especially at night before falling asleep and in the morning after awakening. These are times when they are naturally in a relaxed state. This is especially helpful for the "difficulty falling asleep" symptom characteristic of anxiety and the "global insomnia" symptom associated with a high risk of suicide. It gives individuals an opportunity to use the time spent in bed when they are unable to sleep. The relaxation step of visualization may actually help them to fall asleep. But even if they do not sleep, they will feel relaxed while concentrating on scenes in which they are calm, successful, and happy.

4. Teaching the Use of Affirmations

Affirmations work like visualizations, but they are verbal statements rather than images. The author of <u>Creative Visualization</u>, Shakti Gawain (1978) writes "An affirmation is a strong, positive statement that something is <u>already</u> so. It is a way of making firm that which you are imaging."

Gawain's book gives a number of examples of affirmations that would be helpful to persons with anxiety:

1. *Everything is coming to me easily and effortlessly.*
2. *Everything I need is already within me.*
3. *I love and appreciate myself just as I am.*
4. *I am whole and complete in myself.*
5. *I am always in the right place at the right time, successfully engaged in the right activity.*

6. *It's okay for me to have fun and enjoy myself and I do.*
7. *I am relaxed and centered - I have plenty of time for everything.*
8. *I now enjoy everything I do.*
   (Gawain, 1978, pp. 22-23)

Gawain gives many other examples of affirmations for a wide variety of potentially stressful situations. It could be performance anxiety in academics, sports, work, financial difficulties, or stress arising from difficulties in interpersonal relations. Students can even be encouraged to write an affirmation of their own concerning problems they want resolved in their lives.

The particular strength of affirmations is that students are able to use them at times when it is impossible to use other techniques. You do not have to put yourself in a state of relaxation in order to use affirmations. You can just say these statements any time you need to (e.g., right before a test) or any time you want to (e.g., while waiting for a bus).

Personally, I find writing affirmations to be helpful. The process of moving my hand and seeing the words on the page has a powerful effect. It helps me to concentrate, something we all find hard to do when we are anxious. I can write two or three affirmations over and over again while I am stuck somewhere waiting, and it gives me something positive to do. The calming effect of doing this simple repetitive act with its potential for a positive outcome by itself reduces the anxiety that can arise in the course of everyday life.

Two of the three long-term predictors of suicide are hopelessness and suicidal ideation (frequent thoughts of committing suicide) . What better way to combat hopelessness than by strong, positive statements? What better way to combat intrusive ideas about killing yourself than by writing affirmations (firm statements) about positive things happening in your life?

5. Teaching that alcohol and drug abuse is an ineffective means of self-treating anxiety

Today's parents are frightened their teenagers may begin to experiment with drugs and alcohol. What they may not see is that this behavior is often an attempt to self-treat anxiety. Adolescents who have both depression and anxiety may not be able to accidentally discover a treatment for the depression but will discover that alcohol relieves anxiety. I wish to emphasize that although alcohol does reduce the symptoms of anxiety, it is itself a depressive drug -- it makes the depression worse. If depressed and anxious adolescent and young adults self-medicate with alcohol, they will end up trading reduced anxiety now for greater depression later. Because alcohol gives people an immediate and temporary lift it is hard to convince depressed adolescents that they are actually making the depression worse. Their solution to any new low is to get high again. Others may recognize the self-destructive nature of their behavior, but persons who abuse alcohol and drugs may only see that they are getting some relief from discomfort.

I hope I will not be misunderstood. I realize not everyone who abuses alcohol or becomes addicted to drugs does so because they are anxious and/or depressed people who self-medicate their condition. Researchers alert us to the number of previously not depressed people who develop depression as a result of abusing alcohol and other depressive drugs.   It is important to make a distinction between   people with an underlying depression and/or anxiety disorder versus people who become depressed from using and abusing drugs. We must be careful to treat these two groups differently. Severely anxious and depressed adolescents may need antidepressant medication, but the abusive person may simply need to stop taking the drugs.

Furthermore, mental health professionals now distinguish two types of alcoholism.   Adolescent onset patients have this condition before age 20. It is highly genetic.   These alcoholics have differences in their serotonin levels and do not respond as well to the 12-step program.   Adult onset patients develop their illness after age 20.   This condition is an interplay of both genetic predisposition and abusive behavior.   They respond well to the 12-step program.   Alcoholics Anonymous still is the most effective treatment for these clients.

An important part of any class to help young people today should include a component about alcohol and drugs. The difficulty lies in finding an approach that will have an effect on behavior. While I don't know of any approach that has proven to be successful, perhaps you do. Or maybe your school system is already using one that is helpful. There are indications that the use of street drugs has declined with efforts to tell the whole truth about their negative effects. Similarly, efforts to change the image of drug use from one of glamour, adventure, and fun, to a more accurate image of increased dependency and depression, are also helpful. Educators know that teaching methods which engage students in discussion rather than passively receiving information produces a greater impact on behavior. Methods that combine all these approaches would likely have some success.

THE USE OF PRESCRIPTION DRUGS FOR ANXIETY

The antidepressants used to treat the type of anxiety that responds to medicine are the MAO inhibitors and the SSRIs. The following chapter on medications describes these in detail.

It was stated earlier that although antidepressants are proving to be effective for adults, their efficacy for treatment of adolescent depression is not clear. Their efficacy for treatment of anxiety in adolescents is also unclear. Medications for teens may be helpful (perhaps especially when panic attacks are frequent), but they need to be used cautiously with this age group. Like the treatment of depression, non-medication methods need to be the key component in a program to help young people cope with anxiety.

Offering an elective class to any interested student would provide an inexpensive way of treating mild to moderate forms of anxiety. It would also augment the therapy and/or medication that a specialist would provide for someone who has a serious problem with this disorder. A course that actually provides treatment is a very different approach from what has been done in the past. Hotlines have not worked. (Someone who is serious about attempting suicide is more likely to reach for a bottle of pills or a gun than a telephone.) Educational programs that only increase awareness have not worked. Giving information does not necessarily translate into changed behavior the way skills training does. Providing information on how to obtain help does not translate into people actually going out to seek help when they need it.

Actual treatment that is easily accessible and affordable is essential. An elective class that provides treatment for two clusters of symptoms of depression, the distorted thinking (cognitive therapy), and the problems with everyday relationships (interpersonal skills training), as well as treatment for anxiety (described by the five non-medication techniques in this chapter) has real potential to help young people.

I recognize not everyone who commits suicide is depressed or anxious, but these two conditions are associated with the majority of these deaths. Those who wish to work toward suicide prevention are putting their efforts today into increasing the number of persons getting treatment for these conditions. Using proven methods and techniques that have a high likelihood of reducing anxiety and depression, and formulating a curriculum for an elective class offer the best hope for treating large numbers of young people today. Burns' Ten Days to Self-Esteem is the kind of text that has already *proven* to be effective for groups of depressed young people.

THE ROLE OF MEDICATION

I used to think that doctors discovered the nature of an illness and then chemists designed a medicine to treat it. I have since learned that often medical discoveries are like any other discovery; they are lucky accidents. Sometimes after a substance is found which reduces the symptoms of an illness, scientists will then set out to learn how the medicine works. During this process they begin to learn more about the nature of the illness itself. For example, the early effective medications for depression were discovered between 1949 and 1956. But it is only in recent years that scientists are beginning to unravel the mystery behind these conditions.

LITHIUM:
The Story Behind the Discovery

Lithium helps to stabilize persons by reducing the severity of future recurrences of both the manic and depressive phases of bipolar illness. The history of this medication is fascinating. As Dr. Fieve points out in his classic book, Moodswings, it was not a discovery at all but a rediscovery. We have actually had the treatment for the last 1800 years. Fieve writes:

In the early Greek and Roman tent hospitals some eighteen hundred years ago, the physician Soramus of Ephesus prescribed mineral-water therapy for manic insanity and melancholia. In fact, he advocated in his writing the use of specific alkaline springs for a number of physical and mental illnesses. The tradition persisted for centuries. Today many of these alkaline springs developed by the Romans in southern and western Europe are known to contain high quantities of lithium. (p. 207-208)

Lithium is a perfectly natural substance found on the atomic chart right along with all the other basic elements, such as hydrogen and oxygen.

It gets its name from the Greek word for stone (lithos) because it is usually found in stone - mineral rock. It is also found in mineral waters and in some plant, animal, and human tissues. Historically, lithium has been used to treat a variety of conditions. Fieve writes that one century ago it was used to treat gout, rheumatism, and many other physical as well as mental diseases. Lithium salts, when added to uric acid had been used to dissolve kidney stones. I personally find the connection between rheumatism and lithium interesting. I know a number of persons with depression who also are plagued with arthritic pain, swelling, and crippling. One friend who now takes lithium for his bipolar illness has experienced significant improvement in his arthritis.

Additionally, there is a connection between the treatment of bipolar illness and the treatment of seizure disorder. In the first part of this century, lithium bromide was used to treat epilepsy. As more effective medications were developed to control seizures, the use of lithium for epilepsy was discontinued. Now the connection between treatment of epilepsy and bipolar illness is again emerging. Doctors today are finding that two medications developed for the treatment of epilepsy can be helpful to some persons with bipolar illness. These medicines, carbamazepine and valproic acid, are sometimes used by patients who do not tolerate lithium. Most often these medications are used in combination with lithium to produce greater stability in a patient's moodswings.

The story of lithium's specific use to control bipolar illness is a combination of both good luck and unfortunate coincidence. Fieve writes that in 1949 the Australian psychiatrist John F. Cade suspected the urea found in the urine of manic patients to be the toxin which created the manic state. To test his hypothesis he decided to inject guinea pigs with uric acid. He needed a soluble salt to add to this acid. When he injected the lithium urate into the guinea pigs they did not become manic as he had hypothesized. Instead they became lethargic. This also occurred when he injected the guinea pigs with lithium carbonate alone. Based on these findings, he then gave lithium carbonate to ten manic patients. They all experienced positive calming effects. Cade reported these findings.

The unfortunate coincidence which prevented the use of lithium from being of help to patients with bipolar illness also occurred in the late 1940s. In the United States, lithium chloride was being sold in stores as a salt substitute for persons who needed a sodium-free diet. Obviously, some of the persons who were buying lithium to season their food were people with heart and kidney disease. We now know that people who take lithium need to have salt (sodium chloride) in their diet in order to excrete lithium. Without sodium, the kidney conserves lithium and people can become lithium toxic, which is why these people died. When several deaths with these patients were reported in 1949, lithium was quickly taken off the market.

These deaths caused the American medical community to become extremely cautious about further use of lithium. It was the Danish psychiatrist Mogens Schou who began in 1954 to develop the use of lithium for the treatment of manic-depressive illness. In 1958 the use of lithium was studied in New York State and later in Texas. After more than a decade of study in the United States, it was finally approved by the FDA in 1970. As Dr. Fieve points out in his book, this is "twenty years after its discovery. " (p.211).

Proponents of lithium do not claim that it can prevent all future manic or depressive episodes or that there are no side effects. Bipolar illness is a serious condition and moodswings do still occur for many patients. Side effects such as hand tremors, nausea, and diarrhea are possible. However, many bipolar patients experience dramatic positive results from its use and regard lithium as a truly remarkable medicine for their condition. They and many others are grateful to Dr. Modes Schou for his pioneer work in proving that this medicine works.

Lithium for Young Patients

Psychiatrists estimate that anywhere from one-fourth to one-half of young people whose symptoms indicate depression are really suffering from bipolar illness. These children have symptoms you will recognize if you read Ben's Story. They include stomach aches, headaches, dizziness, bed-wetting, and difficulty concentrating on schoolwork. The children often are phobic. Parents and teachers report bursts of aggressiveness and frantic activity alternating with periods of sluggishness. Sometimes these children are helped during these early stages of their condition by the use of some kinds of antidepressants, since their first symptoms point to depression. When lithium is used with the antidepressants, the lithium appears to reduce the bodily complaints experienced by the children, and the antidepressant reduces their irritability. What happens during adolescence? Undiagnosed and untreated, these young people with bipolar illness are often described as having a behavioral disorder or a character disorder. Their impulsive pleasure seeking behavior alternates with sullen moods. They typically do not respond well to tricyclic antidepressants. But if the clients and the families are willing to give lithium enough time to produce its stabilizing effects, their response to lithium is often remarkable.

The Use of Lithium as a Maintenance Medicine for Bipolar Illness

If the person is not experiencing an acute problem with either mania or severe depression, lithium alone is sometimes used. But psychiatrists today are finding that many patients cannot remain stable with lithium alone. Like patients with epilepsy who often need two medications to prevent or decrease the number of seizures, bipolar clients often need both lithium and Depakene (valproic acid; divalproex) or lithium and Tegretol (carbamazepine) to prevent or reduce the severity of their moodswings. Furthermore, like some persons with epilepsy who require three medications to manage their seizures, some bipolar patients who are not stabilized by either lithium and Depakene or lithium and Tegretol are helped when lithium and Depakene and Tegretol are prescribed.

Use of Other Medications for Acute Episodes of Mania or Depression

Lithium, which helps to stabilize temperament by preventing future moodswings, usually does not work quickly enough to be useful during an acute attack. Bipolar patients who experience mania will need antipsychotic/neuroleptics medicines such as Mellaril, Thorazine, or Trilafon or many others. These medicines are discontinued by many patients soon after the manic episode subsides.

During a swing down into severe depression, bipolar patients will likely benefit from one of the four classes of anti-depressants: a tricyclic such as Tofranil (imipramine), a MAO inhibitor such as Nardil or Parnate, a SSRIs such as Prozac (fluoxetine), and the fourth type of antidepressant, Wellbutrin (bupropion). These medicines too will be discontinued for some patients with bipolar illness soon after the depressive symptoms subside.

Importance of Continuing Maintenance Medication for Bipolar Clients

There are several reasons why it is essential to continue lithium and/or Depakene or Tegretol as an ongoing treatment for bipolar illness. (Since lithium has become the most widely used medicine for decades in the treatment of this illness and is sometimes the only medicine needed to produce stability, I will refer only to lithium when describing why it is important not to discontinue using maintenance medication during periods of stability.)

Bipolar patients who stop lithium can become highly unstable, often more unstable than they were before starting the medicine.

This is not a negative statement indicating that lithium can cause this instability. It is more a reflection on how essential the medicine is for bipolar patients who need it.

Discontinuation of lithium can sometimes interfere with the ability of the person to benefit from the medicine once it is started again.

Some persons who have been stabilized (sometimes for years) on lithium decide for one reason or another to go off the medicine. Some of these people do not experience the same stability when they resume taking lithium as they had before. This phenomena is called "Withdrawal Induced Refractory," meaning that stopping the medication caused the person to become non-responsive to the medicine in the future. Although lithium typically takes time to become effective, and one does not expect to see restabilization for many months, some unfortunate persons who stop lithium can retake it again for years and still not have the same level of stability they had during the many years they took it the first time.

Lithium dramatically decreases the likelihood a bipolar patient will commit suicide.

Bipolar illness is a serious form of depression. The suicide rate among these patients is nearly 20 percent. When lithium is effective in preventing further episodes of moodswings, patients feel less helpless and less hopeless about their condition. It is not surprising that it can help to prevent suicide.

With these powerful reasons for staying on lithium, why would a bipolar client want to discontinue taking it? The reasons are:

1. *After stabilization, the person may begin to believe that they really do not have bipolar illness after all.*

2. *Some bipolar clients use the early stage of manic highs to do productive work.*

3. *Weight gain occurs for some patients.*

4. *Other side effects, such as interference with concentration or fatigue, trouble the client.*

The physicians who are most successful in helping bipolar clients always address these issues. For example, the problems with concentration, memory, and fatigue can be reduced by:

1. *taking all of the lithium at bedtime rather than throughout the day,*

2. *keeping the thyroid level in the high normal range by taking synthroid if necessary,*

3. *taking folic acid either by itself or as part of a multiple vitamin.*

Clients need support if they are to stay on lithium. This can come from family and friends, but an important addition to this is a manic-depressive support group. Whatever the source of support, persons with bipolar illness need to confront the effect that their illness can have on themselves and their family. They also need support in a daily regimen that includes exercise, a healthy diet and good sleep habits (see appendix).

New Findings Regarding the Medicines for Bipolar Illness

Physicians are becoming increasingly cautious when prescribing tricyclic antidepressants to persons with bipolar illness. Tricyclics are very effective medicines, especially for major depression, but there is some evidence that their use can increase the likelihood of "rapid cycling" (four or more episodes of mania or depression in a year). There is also concern that tricyclics can, at least temporarily, prevent a bipolar patient from experiencing the benefits of stabilization in those cases when lithium is used after the tricyclic. Since patients usually experience several bouts of depression before a manic episode and since patients often seek help when depressed and do not seek help when beginning a manic high, it was not uncommon in the past for the bipolar aspect of this depressive condition to go undetected for many years. Consequently, it was not unusual for lithium to be prescribed long after treatment by a tricyclic medication. More research is needed to discover if previous treatment with antidepressants interferes with the general efficacy of lithium in some persons with bipolar illness. Certainly, concomitant tricyclic antidepressants can interfere with lithium effectiveness if it is producing rapid cycling or mania.

The possible problems induced by tricyclics for people with bipolar illness is still one more reason why physicians are likely to prescribe one of the new SSRIs, such as Prozac. Since one-third of all people with serious depression have bipolar illness, cautious physicians realize that even though they may only see the patients in a down cycle, there may be an up cycle as well to their mood disorder.

MAO inhibitors are prescribed for patients during an acute episode of depression when the symptoms fit the category of atypical depression. They are usually used when other antidepressants have not worked. When they succeed where other medicines have not, it is like a miracle for the patient. Like all other antidepressants, MAO inhibitors can trigger mania in a patient with bipolar illness. It is unclear at this point whether MAO inhibitors are worse in that respect than others, but the problem does exist. Careful observation by health care professionals with insight from the family or friends of the client is very important.

Another current finding relates to dosage. A physician's monitoring of the level of lithium in a patient's blood has been focused in the past on maintaining a therapeutic level defined as .8 to 1.2. Dr. Modnes Schou's continued research into the efficacy of lithium reports that levels of .5 to .8 may actually be just as effective for most clients. Furthermore, levels as low as .3 can be helpful to elderly clients who do not metabolize medications as effectively as do younger patients.

Why is it so Important to Treat Persons with Bipolar Illness?

Physicians have reported that persons with bipolar illness experience some of the most painful depressions. These depressions are especially characterized by an inability to concentrate, a lack of ability to enjoy life, and thoughts of killing themselves.

Since bipolar patients usually have several bouts of depression before having an episode of mania, physicians often treat these clients for depression only. When the mania begins, many bipolar clients will self-medicate with alcohol (a depressant drug) as a means of calming themselves down. It is not surprising that 60 percent of bipolar patients are alcoholics. Since alcohol makes one less inhibited, it is a danger for anyone with frequent thoughts of suicide.

Mania is described as feeling high, and a time when the person eats and sleeps little. It sounds great, but the reality is that persons with bipolar illness suffer as much during their manic phases as they do when depressed. I learned about this not only from my experience with Ben, but unexpectedly from one experience of my own.

During the first years after Ben's death, I went through profound grief (a reactive depression). I had low energy, headaches, decreased ability to concentrate, intense sadness. Three years after his death, I volunteered to participate in a nationwide cancer prevention research project. Oncologists were attempting to discover if the drug tamoxifen would be effective in preventing breast cancer for women with specific risk factors. Soon after beginning the medication, I experienced an elevated mood and a decreased need to eat and sleep. One month after starting the medication, I reported these effects to the nurse working on the research project. Realizing that people often experience side effects when starting a medication and these effects often subside over time, I agreed to continue with the drug. However, I did warn her that if the side effects persisted for a long time or became more severe, I would stop the medication.

My elevated mood and decreased appetite appeared wonderful, especially to all of my friends who were envious of my weight loss and enjoyed my highly spirited conversation. What is hard to explain is the discomfort I was experiencing, especially during the nights when I got little sleep.

During the stages of grief following Ben's death, I often had difficulty sleeping. But the sleeplessness then was not as painful as it was during this manic episode. The only way I can begin to describe it is to say that I was excessively restless and just could not tolerate being in my body. I clearly remember the last night I was on the tamoxifen study. Perhaps I slept a total of one hour, but I cannot really be sure if I was able to sleep at all that night. I recall seeing the minutes slowly going by. I could not wait until 5 a.m. when I could get up and start working to take my mind off my discomfort.

Unlike people who suffer from manic episodes as part of their bipolar illness, I did not feel helpless about my situation. I knew that at 8 a.m. I could call the nurse to inform her I was discontinuing the medication. I realized that the effects of the medicine would gradually subside and I would again be able to sleep more normally. And unlike those who suffer from bipolar illness, my manic episode was not followed by the plunge into a painful depression.

Maintenance Medication for Frequent Recurring Unipolar Depression

Lithium is now found to be helpful to prevent or reduce the severity of future episodes of recurrent unipolar depression. There are two reasons why physicians consider its use. First, although antidepressants alone are very helpful during an acute bout of depression, they are discontinued after the depression subsides. If the depression is only a single episode or if the episodes are infrequent, the occasional use of an antidepressant may handle the problem. Unfortunately, for a substantial number of persons, episodes of unipolar depressions occur frequently. Lithium offers some protection against these future episodes.

Approximately one-third of persons with unipolar illness have frequently recurring episodes and will respond to lithium. Some researchers call these patients Unipolar II and believe them to have a form of bipolar illness. I personally believe that many people with Unipolar II are dysthymic most of the time. Their hypomanic cycles get them into what persons without depression experience as "feeling normal," and their depressive periods are very painful. Giving a stabilizing medication to Unipolar II patients reduces unnecessary suffering.

Second, taking lithium may decrease the likelihood of suicide for persons with unipolar depression, just as it has for those persons with bipolar illness, who become more stabilized with its use. One fact stands out in this regard. The two major classes of antidepressants (the tricyclic and MAO inhibitors) were developed in the mid 1950's. If antidepressants protected patients from suicide, one would expect the suicide rate to have declined as more depressed persons use these medicines. Unfortunately, the rate of suicide has not shown a substantial decline in the past decades, and the rate among young people has dramatically increased. Although the use of antidepressants has not increased the suicide rate, neither have they offered protection. Lithium is a medication that has decreased the likelihood that people with bipolar illness will kill themselves.

This issue is complex. Because suicide rates are affected by multiple factors (including cultural and methodologies used in assessing the rates) it has been difficult to determine if any medicine actually decreases the rates of suicide in persons with unipolar illness. Some research has shown antidepressants are equal to lithium for the maintenance treatment of unipolar depression. In the past there has also been some hesitancy to use lithium to prevent frequent recurrences of unipolar depression because there were fears it would adversely affect kidney function. Dr. Schou and others have carefully followed patients who have taken lithium for as many as twenty to thirty years and have not found a basis for concern. It is true that anyone who already has kidney disease may not be able to use lithium, but these patients cannot use salt either. There was one incident of a seventy-two year old male who developed kidney failure after being on lithium. This instance may be merely a coincidence since kidney disease is not uncommon and is on the rise worldwide. To be cautious, physicians monitor kidney function routinely for patients who take lithium.

TRICYCLIC ANTIDEPRESSANTS

The Story Behind the Discovery

The discovery of tricyclics did not initially involve psychiatry but developed in a roundabout way. Fieve writes that a French surgeon wanted to prevent surgical shock. He tried an antihistamine which did not have the results he wanted but did produce a calming effect on the patient. Other doctors wished to use medicines that would work like an antihistamine to help their surgical patients, so chemists began to create similar medicines. The result was chlorpromazine, a medication that is ultimately helpful in treating schizophrenia. Chemists often design medicines that are more effective and have fewer side effects by altering or adding to the chemical formulation of existing medicines. A Swiss chemist attempting to improve chlorpromazine produced Tofranil (imipramine). Tofranil is not effective for the treatment of schizophrenia, but it did relieve the symptoms of depression.

In short, a French surgeon's use of an antihistamine to prevent surgical shock prompted a Swiss chemist's attempt to improve on chlorpromazine, which produced the antidepressant imipramine. These lucky accidents show how many significant discoveries are made. Someone is looking for one thing and they come upon something else. Wasn't Christopher Columbus searching for the Indies when he stumbled on the Western Hemisphere? Improvements and advancement in science and medicine occur when open minded people discover something other than what they set out to find, and recognize the value of what they have stumbled upon.

The Use of Tricyclic Medications

One of the most practical ways to describe the different classes of antidepressants is to correlate them with the type of depressive symptoms they are most effective in treating. Tricyclic antidepressants are especially helpful to patients with major depression. The word "major" describes **typical** cases of serious depression. It defines patients who:

1. *experience low mood which is not relieved by any cheerful changes in the environment,*
2. *fall asleep without trouble, wake early and cannot get back to sleep,*
3. *feel worse in the morning,*
4. *have decreased appetite resulting in weight loss,*
5. *have difficulty concentrating,*
6. *have depressions that occur in discrete episodes.*

Tricyclic medications are helpful for major depression and have a success rate of at least 80 percent. There are many tricyclics on the market, and physicians may need to try several before discovering exactly which one will work best for a particular client. There is no way to know in advance or to test a patient to discover which tricyclic will prove to be most helpful. The oldest one and the one that has had the most rigorous investigation through the years is Tofranil (imipramine).

A tricyclic (as the word tricycle denotes) has a "three-ring chemical structure" (5/4/87, p. 52). Many physicians and their patients feel comfortable with the use of tricyclics, such as imipramine, because the medication has been around for almost forty years. The long-term effects of taking this medication have been studied. To date there is no evidence of problems resulting from continued use. Also, the extensive research on imipramine over the years has repeatedly proven its efficacy. Just a few years ago it was part of the large, multi-site collaborative study by the National Institute of Mental Health. The results of the study indicated that a high percentage of patients who received medication combined with short term psychotherapies designed specifically for depression had successful outcomes.

MAO INHIBITORS
The Story Behind the Discovery

The story of the monoamine oxidase (MAO) inhibitors is a tale of still another lucky accident. This time it involved physicians in tuberculosis hospitals. They observed that the antibiotic created for tubercular patients had the effect of improving the mood of those who were depressed.

Monoamine oxidase (MAO) is an enzyme which causes the breakdown of many neurotransmitters once they get to the next neuron. MAO inhibitors prevent the breakdown of the neurotransmitters; thus, it increases the amount of neurotransmitters available in the brain. A tricyclic like imipramine also increases the amount of available neurotransmitters. It does this by preventing norepinephrine from being reabsorbed by presynaptic neurons.

So, in very simplistic terms, the tricyclics work by blocking re-absorption of the messengers by the nerve cells that release them, and the MAO inhibitors work to prevent the breakdown of neurotransmitters by the neurons that receive the message. It may appear as if scientists now "know" how these medicines work, but all that can be said is that although scientists do not fully understand how tricyclics and MAO inhibitors work to relieve depression, these medicines "bolster the actions of serotonin and norepinephrine, two of the chemicals that transmit impulses through the nervous system." (3/26/90, p. 39)

The Use of MAO Inhibitors

Again, the most practical way to begin talking about this class of anti-depressant drug is to describe the type of depression it helps. The term **atypical** depression does not describe a less serious or unusual kind of depression as compared to major depression. Instead, the term "atypical depression" describes patients who:

1. *can be temporarily cheered by a pleasant change in the environment,*

2. *are on an emotional roller -coaster in which praise and attention produce excessive highs and rejection or criticism produce extreme lows,*

3. *overeat and subsequently gain weight,*

4. *oversleep, and even after sleeping as much as twelve or fourteen hours will report feeling tired,*

5. *have decreased energy and lack motivation,*

6. *feel worse at the end of the day,*

7. *are less episodic and may report feeling constantly out of sorts.*

Two of the most commonly prescribed MAO inhibitors are Parnate and Nardil. Everyone experiences various side effects. Nardil usually causes more weight gain (a problem persons with atypical depression, like Ben, already struggle with). Parnate causes more disturbance in sleep patterns (a problem that is troublesome for many people with depression). It is paradoxical that even though MAO inhibitors have a success rate of at least 80 percent for clients with atypical depression, the medicine produces similar symptoms of the condition itself. Success rates for treatment of depression are impressively high, but my experience with Ben has made me aware of the need to be sympathetic and alert to the struggles of patients with the side effects of their treatment.

Selective Serotonin Reuptake Inhibitors

The Story Behind their Development

I know of no lucky accident involving Prozac (fluoxetine), one of the first SSRIs. With the large number of persons suffering from depression and the problems they encounter with side effects from tricyclics and MAO inhibitors, there was a need for medications that patients could and would take more easily. Even though the antidepressants discovered in the 1950's have an impressively high success rate, the efficacy of the tricyclics and MAO inhibitors are irrelevant if patients are unable or unwilling to stay on the medicine.
Tricyclics, for example can cause

dry mouth
headache
sluggishness
dizziness
blurred vision
constipation
memory loss
insomnia
agitation
weight gain

In addition, they can cause blood pressure and heart disturbances. This is especially a problem for older patients.

Often these side effects are mild and go away after a short period of time, but some people are unusually sensitive to them. Typically, about one-third of patients cannot or choose not to tolerate these side effects and discontinue the use of tricyclic medication.

The side effects of MAO inhibitors are much like the side effects from tricyclics. The big difference is that patients taking MAO inhibitors need to restrict their use of:

some foods, e.g. aged cheese,
some medicines, e.g. cold medication,
some drinks, e.g. red wine.

Because of the potentially harmful interactions of these products with an MAO inhibitor, physicians are careful to prescribe them only to clients who are able to follow the restrictions.

In additions to the side effects, tricyclics and MAO inhibitors require a patient to begin with a small dose and only gradually increase it. The therapeutic level is not reached for some time. Consequently, months may go by before the physician can accurately evaluate the suitability of a particular tricyclic or MAO inhibitor for a specific client. People who take Prozac, on the other hand, often get the maximum antidepressant effect from taking just the one 20 mg tablet which is given from the first day of treatment.

When Prozac became available in December of 1987 it soon became known as a wonder drug. It seemed like a wonder drug because it is easier to tolerate for most patients. Prozac, however, is not totally without side effects. The most common include:

headaches
nausea
insomnia
jitteriness
weight loss

It is that last side effect, weight loss, that may particularly explain the willingness of some patients to tolerate the other side effects of Prozac. Most of us are willing to lose a few pounds. In addition, we would rather feel slightly wired than sluggish. The side effects of Prozac are usually temporary, just as they are with other medications. Most people tolerate them well over the short period of time needed for the body to adjust to the medication.

Some Facts about SSRIs

1. SSRIs work like the tricyclics in that they block reabsorption of a neurotransmitter by the nerve cell that <u>releases</u> them. While tricyclics block reabsorption of a number of neurotransmitters, SSRIs work more exclusively on just one type of neurotransmitter -- serotonin. The term SSRIs refers to "selective serotonin reuptake inhibitors."

2. SSRI's help people with bipolar illness and those with atypical depression in a way that is similar to MAO inhibitors. Because there are no dietary restrictions with SSRIs, they are easier to use for these patients.

3. It is important to keep in mind that SSRIs are no more effective for depression than the tricyclics and MAO inhibitors. The older medications have a success rate of at least 80 percent. The success rate for the new SSRIs is not higher than the older medications.

4. Because SSRIs are easier to tolerate for most patients, they may be especially important for the elderly, whose bodies often have difficulty processing medication.

5. It is important to have normal levels of serotonin. Low serotonin levels are a predictor of suicidality because low levels of that particular neurotransmitter are associated with impulsivity and aggression.

Some Specifics about Prozac, Zoloft, Paxil, and Effexor

Prozac (fluoxetine) is a more wide range medication than some of the other SSRIs. Case reports indicate it may also be useful for patients suffering certain anxiety disorders, obsessive compulsive conditions, bulimia, kleptomania, obesity, addiction, and borderline personality disorder.

Zoloft (sertraline) works more on serotonin than Prozac but not as exclusively as does Paxil. Research indicated that it is helpful to patients with major depression.

Paxil (paroxetine) works exclusively on serotonin. Consequently, it is especially helpful for people whose depression manifests itself as symptoms of irritability and anger. There is also some indications that Paxil may be less likely to switch a person with bipolar illness from the depressive phase to mania.

Effexor (venlafaxine) is one of the newest SSRIs. Current hypotheses suggest that Effexor may work by two potential mechanisms of action, inhibiting the reuptake of both serotonin and norepinephrine.It may work as well for people suffering from severe typical depression as does the older tricylic, while producing fewer side affects than they do.

Because SSRIs are relatively new medicines, the long term affects are still not known. Physicians who choose to use them for extended periods will want to routinely reevaluate the long-term usefulness of these medicines for each of their clients.

Rationale for Caution

There is enthusiasm for the relatively low side effects of the SSRIs. There is no need to restrict the use of certain products when taking a SSRI as is required with the MAO Inhibitors. SSRIs users do not need to have their blood levels monitored as is done when taking lithium. SSRIs may seem like dream medications, but caution is warranted.

First, tricyclics and MAO inhibitors have been around for forty years and thus have a track record, which SSRIs do not. We cannot possibly know the long term consequences of using SSRIs . There does not appear to be any reason to suggest that use over long periods of time will prove to be problematic, especially since the other antidepressants have not. But until the data actually exists, no one can be certain.

Perhaps an even more interesting question is, will SSRIs continue to have an antidepressant effect for those clients who require on-going treatment? Or, will it become less effective with continued use? Until patients have been on a medication for many years, no one can say with certainty what the long term effect will be.

Third, no drug works perfectly for every one. Like any other medication, it is possible to have a paradoxical effect (patients getting worse rather than better). Furthermore, some SSRI users report feeling restless and some have tremors.

Most depression is treated by non-psychiatric physicians (e.g. internists, family practitioners, etc.). Since SSRIs are easier to prescribe, they tend to have greater success with it. But SSRIs, like any other medication, can produce adverse reactions.

Because depression is such a painful condition, compassionate doctors are willing to prescribe medications like Prozac, which has few side effects and helps most of those who take it. But unless they insist that patients produce some data on their moods, they may open themselves up to the same type of criticism with SSRIs as doctors experienced when valium and librium were prescribed widely for anxiety during the 1960's and 1970's.

Personal Comments Regarding Prozac

Prozac is a medication recommended for persons whose symptoms are that of atypical depression and who are not likely to follow the restrictions necessary for treatment with an MAO inhibitor. Ben's symptoms fit the diagnosis of atypical depression, and he was unlikely to stay away from pizza, lasagna, tacos and other foods prepared with cheese. Prozac was also ideal for Ben because it is recommended for patients with panic attacks, and it would not exacerbate Ben's weight problem. Prozac is also used for some clients who are phobic. Ben appears to have been an ideal candidate for treatment with Prozac.

My son died while taking Prozac. Do I blame his death on this medication? My answer today is "probably not," but six months after Ben's death, after hearing of reports of cases of persons using the medication becoming manic or suicidal, I did become concerned about the safety of this new medication.

Over time I have learned that Prozac, like any other antidepressant, must be prescribed differently for bipolar patients than for unipolar patients. There is a fundamental difference in the length of time a typical patient with unipolar depression will stay on the antidepressant, compared to the length of time a patient with bipolar illness usually needs to take that type of medicine. Persons with unipolar depression need to stay on their antidepressant for many months after their spirits rise. This is mandatory because depressive illness affects the body in many different ways. A change in mood is one of the first changes to be experienced after the medicine is started. But the depressive illness itself still affects people after their mood rises. Stopping the medicines before they are completely well increases the likelihood they will feel depressed again soon because their bodies are not yet fully recovered from the illness. It may be analogous to stopping an antibiotic prematurely because one begins to feel better. Antibiotics need to be taken for the full seven to ten days as prescribed by the doctor. Likewise, antidepressants need to be taken for several months (perhaps as many as nine months) after the patient's mood rises for persons who have <u>unipolar</u> depression.

Bipolar patients, on the other hand, typically will discontinue the use of one of these four classes of antidepressants a few weeks after their spirits rise. This is done in order to prevent them from being pushed into a manic episode. It is valuable for the physician to have as a working hypothesis the possibility that any depressed patient may turn out to actually have bipolar illness. This involves being conscientious about carefully following the mood cycles of anyone on an antidepressant. The best way to do this is to have the person, and sometimes the family or a close friend, keep a mood chart. This is simply done by scoring their mood each day from: + 10 for extreme high, 0 for normal mood,   - 10 for deep low.

This easy system can detect moodswings and provide the kind of objective information that will save time, money, and unnecessary pain for everyone.

WELLBUTRIN

Wellbutrin (bupropion) became available in the summer of 1989. It is chemically unrelated to any other class of antidepressant. The 1993 Physicians Desk References states that "The neurochemical mechanism of the antidepressant effect of buproprion is not known." In a recent lecture, Dr. Frederick Goodwin stated that Wellbutrin likely acts on dopamine. It produces a stimulating effect on the central nervous system. It is helpful to a different group of people than those taking SSRIs.

Young persons with attention deficit hyperactive disorder (ADHD) are typically helped by using Ritalin, a stimulant medication. ADHD is characterized by impulsivity, an inability to concentrate, and overactivity. Stimulant medication improves an ADHD student's ability to focus on a task while not exacerbating the hyperactivity. Ritalin does not cure ADHD, any more than insulin cures diabetes. It only allows the client to manage a condition for which there is no cure.

Wellbutrin is being used as an alternative to Ritalin for students with ADHD. There is some enthusiasm for its use, but it is too soon to know if Wellbutrin will prove to be a more desirable medicine for ADHD than Ritalin. Since some children with ADHD are actually suffering from the manifestations of bipolar illness, Wellbutrin may prove to be a useful treatment. Wellbutrin has been found helpful for some children and adolescents who have both ADHD and depression symptoms, but may *not* be helpful for persons with high level anxiety.

Wellbutrin is recommended for bipolar patients and for clients with major depression. Initial data indicate it may have "less tendency to produce hypomania and mania than other antidepressants and therefore may be especially useful for patients with bipolar depression who often get manic when treated with antidepressants."

The side effects of Wellbutrin include: restlessness, agitation, insomnia, headache, nausea, vomiting, and rash. This list is not that different from what is found with the other antidepressants. Like the SSRIs, Wellbutrin does not cause weight gain. Initially, patients may even lose a few pounds.

The biggest concern is a risk of seizures. There have been some incidents in which the medication precipitated seizures. It is not a medication that should be prescribed for patients with a known diagnosis of epilepsy, or for those who have brain structural lesions, or those who have eating disorders because people with these problems are at risk for seizures on Wellbutrin.

There are some indications that this stimulant medication may be especially helpful for elderly patients. Wellbutrin is sometimes prescribed to adults along with an SSRI because it may help to counteract the reduced sexually response that can occur with taking an SSRI.

A Personal Note on Wellbutrin

In the summer of 1989, Ben appeared to have been a perfect candidate for Wellbutrin. He had ADHD and was bipolar. However, it became available after Ben's death on May 31.

How would Ben have responded to Wellbutrin if he had had the opportunity to use it? I will never know the answer to that question. I do, however, know how his father responded to it when it was prescribed for his depression in 1990. You will recall that the response of a close relative (with a naturally high likelihood of having a similar body chemistry) is a good predictor of a patient's response to the same medicine. Garry's response to Wellbutrin was not successful. This has taught me that no matter how ideal candidates may originally seem to be for a particular medicine, there is no guarantee that it will work for them. In 1994 I now know why Ben probably would not have responded well to Wellbutrin. Ben had a serious anxiety disorder.

NEW VERSUS OLD MEDICATION

Advertising and commercials have conditioned us to equate the newness of a product with improvement. It has gotten to the point that established products almost have to claim they are in some way new and improved if they are to continue to hold their customers. The term "tried and true" does not hold the same meaning in our era of rapid change as it did when change was less dramatic and ongoing.

The older antidepressants have been around for nearly forty years. The tricyclics are still very effective medications for some people with severe cases of major depression. MAO inhibitors are still effective for some persons with depression when all other medicines have failed to help.

Lithium was used 1800 years ago to treat or promote the physical and mental well being of patients. Working on the second messenger system, it is the only medications that can function as an amplifier when the person is depressed and as a minimizer when the person become hypomanic or manic. Lithium also augments the effectiveness of other antidepressants. Some psychiatrists are so convinced of the augmentative value of lithium, that they will routinely give it to all their unipolar patients along with the antidepressant and then remove it once the antidepressant has relieved the symptoms.

The new SSRI's will most likely prove to be a great blessing for millions. It use to be said that only one out of four persons with severe depressive illness sought treatment for their illness. In recent years, the figure comes closer to one out of two. In part this is a result of efforts by organizations like the National Institute of Mental Health which has worked to raise the public awareness of the symptoms of depression. Undoubtedly it is also due in part to the development of the new, easier to tolerate, SSRIs.

When starting an antidepressant, patients will likely experience a jagged rather than a straight-line improvement in their symptoms. They may feel better, then worse, better, then worse. But their course will be upwards over time, if the medicine is effective for them. Only a trial of medication will actually tell what works most effectively for a specific person. Careful follow-up with a physician is essential.

Each year pharmaceutical companies produce more new medications that have proven, in controlled trials, to be efficacious. Put on the market for use by the general public, they may prove over time to be effective for a large number of people. However, it is important to remember that any medication can cause unexpected or unwanted effects. For example medicines that generally cause mood stability can cause instability for a particular person. No one can predict with certainty how any medicine will work for a specific patient.

Adderall is indicated as an integral part of a total treatment program for attention deficit disorder with hyperactivity. *Warning:* this is an amphetamine and has a high potential for abuse. Long term effect of amphetamines in children have not been well established.

Lamitcal (lamotrigine) It may have antidepressant properties in bipolar I and II depression, including in patients resistant to standard mood stabilizers and antidepressants.

Luvox (fluvoxamine maleate) It is a SSRI but of a new series, thus it is chemically unrelated to the other SSRI's. It is especially helpful for people who suffer from obsessive compulsive disorder.

Neurontin (gabapentin) Early research indicates two-thirds of bipolar I and II patients sustained mood-stabilizing effects. It has a good side effect profile.

Remeron (mirtazapine) It functions like the SSRI's, but does not cause the sexual dysfunction that a minority of patients experience as a side effect. Its pharmacological action includes improving activity of norepinephrine and serotonin.

Revia (naltrexone) It is purported to work for people who are both alcoholic and depression. It is works on the brain morphine systems. It may be helpful for adolescent-onset alcoholism. NOTE: Acamprosate may come on the American market in the future. It also may be helpful for alcohol addictions, a problem so common for patients with bipolar illness.

Risperdal (resperedone) It was developed as a front-line medication treatment option for psychotic disorders but is proving to be helpful in producing stability for some bipolar patients who do not respond to lithium monotherapy.

Tenex (guanfacine hydrocholride)   is indicated in the management of hypertension in adults.   Because the safety and effectiveness in children has not been demonstrated the manufacture does not recommend the use of Tenex in this age group.   However in the future this medicine may prove to be helpful for youngsters with early onset bipolar illness.

Topamax (topiramate) is indicated as adjunctive therapy for treatment of adults with partial onset seizures. Some clinician are finding this medications useful as adjunctive therapy for bipolar patients. It often reduces the carbohydrate craving produced by other mood stabilizers.

Zyprexa (olanzapine)   It is a new front-line medication for treatment of psychotic disorder which produces fewer side effects than older anti-psychotic medication. It pay prove to be helpful to schizo-affective patients. It does not have the side affect of reducing bone marrow.
Everyone would like a simple way to treat bipolar illness. We have dreams of fining a medicine that has few or very easily managed side effects. We also would love to find a way to determine beforehand exactly what medication will work best for a particular patient. Unfortunately, that ideal may still take years of research or it may remain a goal that will never be reached. We can only hope that someday our dreams will come true.

But one thing is clear. Mental illness left untreated cost twice as much in real dollars as treatment. All other illnesses cost the same whether you treat them or not. Isn't the treatment of mental illness the most cost effective medicine there is?

New Findings for Bipolar Children

The good news is that more is being learned about bipolar illness every day. This chapter will present the important findings of a number of child-psychiatrists who also see a correlation between the symptoms of depression in the bipolar child and the symptoms of other conditions such as ADHD, oppositional defiance, and anxiety. Second, it looks at continuing efforts by psychologist to find the most effect therapies for bipolar illness. Third, it gives further updates on the findings of psychopharmicologist regarding medications. Finally, it suggests the role of current work of molecular biology, neuroscience and genetics in unraveling the mystery of this illness.

In March of 1997 an important conference was, held focusing on Bipolar Disorder in youngster before the age of puberty. Before summarizing the findings which some of the leading researchers presented at the conference, I will present some background which will make their findings more meaningful.

Ben, like most children with bipolar illness, met certain criteria for other conditions. As many as 85% - 90% of prepubertal children who meet criteria for bipolar illness also have symptoms of attention deficit hyperactive disorder (ADHD). Furthermore, bipolar children typically have more of the symptoms of ADHD than do children who have ADHD but are not bipolar.

One way to meet criteria for a diagnosis of ADHD is for the child to display at least six of the nine symptoms that fall under the heading of inattention for a period of at least half a year.

Inattention
a. doesn't pay attention to details or makes careless errors in schoolwork, chores, or activities
b. has problems maintaining attention to tasks or when play
c. has difficulty listening to directions
d. does not complete school assignments, household tasks, or follow instructions
e. is unorganized
f. is hesitant to do tasks that involve concentration; e.g., school assignments, and may try to avoid doing them
g. loses items needed to perform a task- e.g. worksheet or school books, or tools and equipment for doing household chores
h. becomes distracted by external stimuli
i. has problems remembering normal daily tasks

The other way a child could meet the criteria for ADHD is to have at least six of the nine symptoms under the heading of hyperactivity and impulsivity

Hyperactivity
a. has difficulty sitting quietly in a seat or fidgets with hands
b. gets out of the seat in situations such as the classroom at times when others are able to remain seated
c. runs around or climbs in situations where it is not appropriate
d. frequently has difficulty playing quietly

e. activity has a "driven" quality, as if their motor is running
and they can't shut it off
f. extremely talkative

Impulsivity
g. gives an answer before the person is done asking the
question
h. has problems taking turns
i. interrupts others who are talking and/or intrudes into
other children's play

Since a child required only a total of six symptoms to
meet criteria for ADHD, and since bipolar children have more
symptoms of ADHD than children who are ADHD but not
bipolar, I believe that using this symptom list can become part
of the screening for bipolar illness in childhood. It seems
logical that a child whose parents or teachers identify as
having a high number of these symptoms should be referred
for further evaluation by a professional.

Ben had mild symptoms of oppositional defiance
disorder (ODD). The list of the eight symptoms of this
condition is found on page 37. Keep in mind that a child only
needs four of the symptoms to meet criteria for the condition.
Because a majority of children with bipolar illness also meet
criteria for ODD, any parent or teacher who observes these
symptoms in addition to the symptoms of depression and
ADHD may want to refer the child as a possible candidate for
a diagnosis of bipolar illness.

Ben suffered from an anxiety disorder. The six
symptoms of anxiety appear on page 150. Children only need
to have one of these symptoms to meet criteria for this

condition, but the symptom(s) must persist for most of the time during a six month period.

Ben did not have a conduct disorder (CD). This condition is one in which there is a pattern of violating the rights of others. To meet criteria, the child needs to have displayed three of the symptoms in the past year with at least one of these displayed in the last six months.

Aggression
1. bullies others
2. engages in fights
3. uses a weapon to hurt others
4. is cruel to others
5. is cruel to animals
6. steals from others when they are present
7. compels another to engage in sex

Property destruction
8. sets fires
9. non-accidental destruction of property

Stealing or deceiving
10. breaking and entering
11. uses lies to get things or favors from others
12. steals when no one is around

Breaks rules
13. stays out later at night than parents permit
14. ran away from home at least two times
15. school truancy

It is important to keep in mind that many children and adolescents who have a conduct disorder are **not** bipolar.

But in the research that follows you will see that some youngsters who are bipolar also have this condition.

The 1997 NIMH Workshop on Prepubertal Bipolar Disorder

Gabrielle Carlson, M.D. SUNY at Stony Brook, and Dennis Cantewell, UCLA, address the rate of childhood and adolescence mania in the population.

Epidemiological sample 6%
DSM III criteria 7.5% distinct period of mania required
DSM IIIR criteria 10% distinct period of mania not required

Peak age of onset 15-20 years old
50% of youngsters abuse alcohol & drugs

Early onset of bipolar illness increases the risk for substance abuse 22/102 patients with childhood depression made suicide attempts that were reported to parents.   An additional 11/102 patients made unreported attempts

Hypersexuality in childhood in the absence of a history of sexual abuse is almost always attributed to mania.

Dr. Barbara Geller, Washington University: Data from her study of 42 youngsters with bipolar illness, average 9.1 years.

The co-morbid conditions of these children include:
ADHD 85.5%
ODD 83.3%
anxiety disorder 50%

The diagnosis of ADHD was made 3–4 years prior to a diagnosis of bipolar illness. The symptoms found in the youngsters studied by Dr. Geller are:

1. elated mood,
2. grandiosity,
3. dare-devil acts,
4. increased sexuality and
5. racing thoughts

She found *mixed states* mania and depression occurring together in 83% of these children. These youngsters would go instantaneously from laughing to crying. Geller stresses that bipolar children often have a chronic, ongoing mood disorder rather than the distinct episodes more typically found in the adult form of the condition.

Dr. Joseph Biederman, Massachusetts General Hospital: Data on the number of bipolar children with an age of 7 years

The co-morbid conditions of these children include:

1. ADHD 90%
2. conduct disorder 40%

Dr. Biederman notes that children with early onset of ADHD have a 40% risk for alcohol or drug abuse during adolescence. NOTE: Many therapists have concluded that bipolar children should be enrolled in abuse prevention programs because substance abuse has a negative effect on gene expression. Consequently, the prevention of drug abuse in bipolar youngsters may improve their prognosis.

Manic children often experience more physical trauma than other children. On a personal note, remember that Ben had three injuries: he broke his collar bone, had a concussion and broke his arm. All these injuries happened age 4.5–6 years. Dr. Biedeman's observations that bipolar children experience more physical trauma than other children rang true. Dr. Biedeman goes on to report that for some youngsters this physical trauma is followed by an episode of depression.

Upon reviewing the charts of previous patients, Dr. Biederman concluded that the use of tricyclic antidepressants made bipolar children worse. The use of second generation anti-depressants such as prozac, zoloft, paxol, etc., may not cause significant improvement. But that mood stabilizers such a lithium, valproic acid (Depakote), and carbamazepine (Tegretol) may be more helpful. NOTE: We are now in an anticonvulsant renaissance. Some of the new anticonvulsants are proving to be very helpful to people with bipolar illness. Bipolar children in the future will undoubtedly be helped by decreased episodes or longer periods of relative wellness between episodes because of the use of these medications.

ADDITIONAL NOTE: Researchers such as Dr. Hagob Akiskal and Dr. Robert Post have wondered if bupropion (Wellbutrin) may be the stimulant of choice for bipolar youngsters on mood stabilizers who have residual ADHD rather than methylphenidate (Ritalin). Both of these medications are equally effective in treating ADHD, but bupropion has the benefit of being an effective anti-depressant, thus it would be helpful for preventing or treating break-through depression. However, they and other researchers are concerned about the risk of any stimulant medication in bipolar children. Among the risks are possibility of stimulant abuse among adolescents with bipolar illness.

Dr. Hagob Akiskal, University of California, San Diego: Data on Symptoms of children whose parents have bipolar illness and behavioral disorders.

This data was published in 1993. None of the 68 youngsters studied initially had received a diagnosis of mood disorder. But three years later, 27% of these youngsters did receive a diagnosis: 4 had dysthymia, 6 had major depression, 11 had cyclothymic bipolar II, 4 had mania.

Dr. Stan Kutcher, Halifax, Canada: The history of psychiatric disorder in the families of adolescents with mania

30% had first-degree relatives (parent and/or siblings) with major depression
15% had first-degree relatives with bipolar depression
34% had first-degree relatives with anxiety disorder

Adolescents with Bipolar I illness tended to have functioned very well before the onset of illness, whereas adolescents with Bipolar II tended to show disability in school and psychiatric symptoms from an early age.

One study by Duffey indicates that children whose parents were not helped by the use of lithium tended to have psychiatric symptoms and more chronic problems than children whose parents responded to the use of lithium.

Because medication response by relatives tends to predict probable response for new patients, this research would be helpful in deciding to choose an anticonvulsant such as valproic acid (Depakote) for children of lithium non-responding parents.

Dr. Strober, University of California, Los Angeles

4% of persons who experience *adult* onset bipolar illness have first-degree relative with this condition

12% of persons who experience *adolescent* onset bipolar illness have first-degree relative with this condition

30% of persons who experience *prepubertal* onset bipolar illness have first-degree relative with this condition

On a personal note I will be interested to see further research on this. I wonder if other scientists will find even higher percentages.

Dr. Strober made a distinction between children who had an early history of ADHD vs. children with co-morbid condition of conduct disorder and oppositional defiance The latter's response to lithium was extremely slow. Valproic acid seems to work better for these patients and was as effective as lithium in treating patients with mixed states.

Many pediatric psychiatrists agree that parents are often "ahead of pediatricians and adult psychiatrists not only in recognizing bipolar illness symptoms, but also in asking for early and effective pharmacological intervention."

One way for parents to provide treating physicians with important data on their child is to use the Kiddie Life Chart (K-LCM th) Continued use of this chart will also produce the best data from which to determine the effectiveness of treatment.

Dr. Melvin McInnis presented Dr. Raymond DePaula's work at Johns Hopkins

Today's bipolar children tend to experience their illness 10 years earlier than their parents. Youngsters who have Bipolar I illness may become ill as much as 20 years earlier than their parents. Dr. Gershon, in 1987, and Lasch, et al in 1990, coined the term "cohort effect" to describe the finding that in every generation following WWII there is a "higher incidence and earlier age of onset of both unipolar and bipolar affect illness." There is no clear cut explanation for this phenomenon.

It might be related to "anticipation" a term used in genetics to describe the expression of a DNA nucleotide triple repeat sequence for between generations. This means "the repeat of three base pair sequence which comes from a single amino acid."

An example of how anticipation works is found in Huntington's Chorea. The gene for that particular illness is found on the upper portion of chromosome #4. If the infant has 36 triple repeats, it will not get the disorder as an adult. As the number of triple repeats increases, so does the risk of the illness.

If the infant has 40 triple repeats, it is at some risk of not only getting the condition, but of having a more serious case and experiencing symptoms at a younger age. If the infant has 60–80 triple repeats, then they have onset during childhood. Thus a parent may have only 45 repeats but because of genetic anticipation (the expression of DNA nucleotides) the adult might transmit more to their children.

Does anticipation occur in mood disorders such as bipolar illness? Researchers are attempting to answer this question. What is clear is that unipolar and bipolar illness in children was not seen as a problem 20 years ago. Today the incidence and severity of these disorders in childhood and adolescence makes it anything but a rare and insignificant medical condition.

Dr. Pamela Cole, Penn. State University: Data on the development of normal and pathological emotional regulation

Most youngsters have modulated affect.

a. The subgroup with *un*expressed affect has decreased electrodermal and heart rate changes to external stress.
b. The subgroup with expressive and anger-dysregulated response has increased electrodermal and heart rate responses.

Personal note: This data points out an interesting biological factor which underscores the medical nature of bipolar illness, as well as the biological basis for behavior. All too often parents assume they are somehow to blame for the depressed mood and/or angry behavior of their child. It is always enlightening to learn about the biological nature of mood and behavior.

Dr. Michael Potegal, University of Wisconsin, described the characteristic of temper tantrums of children with affect disorders.

Tantrums last longer as the child moves to the 18-30 months old age, but they are still brief. Tantrums associated with whining and crying lasted much longer.

Note: Dr. Arnold Meyersburg suggests this holding procedure. The adult holds the child on his or her lap with the child's back towards the parent and the child's arms crossed in front of them. This prevents the child from striking out at himself or the adults. The child initially attempts to escape and resists by kicking, screaming and/or crying. The adult continues to hold until the outburst ends. This usually takes 30–45 minutes.

When this procedure is used to manage subsequent temper outburst, the tantrum is shortened. The third outbursts may last a matter of just a few minutes. Eventually the child may begin to approach the adults in order to be held and comforted when they experience frustration and anger rather than having a temper tantrum.

All researchers agree

Children and adolescents with bipolar illness are often severely affected by their illness, causing significant disability academically and socially. This in turn causes great distress to everyone in the community, the school, and the family. Without early diagnosis and successful treatment, they are at risk for hurting themselves and/or others.

It behooves parents, school officials and the community to help these youngsters get effective treatment because:

1. decreasing unnecessary suffering for the victim is the humane thing to do
2. decreasing unnecessary problems for others is the socially responsible, wise thing to do
3. early treatment correlates with better prognosis effective treatment is far less expensive than failure to treat psychiatric disorders

Thus, early diagnosis of bipolar and unipolar illness is nothing short of enlightened self-interest.

Psychological Therapies Now Being Researched

I was an elementary education teacher for four years. During the first month of teaching, like most other new teachers, I ran into some discipline problems with my students. The principal gave me a piece of advice that I remember well: "You'll find that everything will go more smoothly once you establish and follow a routine." She was absolutely right. Children have fewer behavioral problems when there is *structure* in their lives. This is particularly true for children who have bipolar illness.

Dr. Fredrick Goodwin notes that people with mood disorders do not possess the requisite degree of flexibility to adapt to environmental change. There are some environmental factors we can not totally control.   Dr. Goodwin cites the effect *circadian rhythms* have on mood. The circadian (clock) systems in the Suprachiasmatic nucleus of the hypothalamus are one of the major regulators of the brain in animals. The gene that regulates this clock has been identified in fruit flies.   The neurotransmitters serotonin, dopamine, and norepinephrine regulate this clock, which is affect by light.

Because of the elliptical pattern of the earth around the sun, the rate of change in ratio of light to dark is not uniform throughout the year. It accelerates in spring and fall. Persons with typical depression (see p. 185) and Bipolar I illness are often more affected by the rate of change. Thus, their moods sometime have seasonal spring or fall patterns.

Some types of depression are affected more by the amount of light.   Persons with bipolar II and others with atypical depression (See p. 187) are more affected this way. They are prone to winter depression and summer hypomania. An estimated 40% of people who have bipolar II illness have seasonal affective disorder.

Broad spectrum light may be an effective way to help bipolar children who experience winter depression. Affective disorder in general is primarily a problem of a central nervous system that is poorly buffered from outside forces.   Broad spectrum light could help mitigate nature's decreased supply of light during winter. Establishment and maintenance of a routine in daily activity is a logical way to increase the buffer of other environmental factors.

Research is now going on at the University of Pittsburgh on Interpersonal and Social Rhythm Therapy.   The subjects of the study include adults who have Bipolar I illness. The goals of the therapy include helping the person find and maintain the right balance of rest, activity and stimulation. It is logical for parents and teachers to take a look at the activity patterns in the child's life and develop and maintain a structure that will support a child whose central nervous system is not well equipped to handle change.

The child's family can not cure the youngster's bipolar illness any more than a child's family can cure their youngster's diabetes. Children with either of these conditions are helped when their parents are willing to learn as much as they can about the nature of the illness, encourage adherence to medication regimes, and support necessary routines to maintain well (exercise, nutritiously balanced diets eaten at a precise time each day, and proper rest). These children are also helped when the family develops a set of behaviors that neither criticizes the child for having the illness nor is overly involved in interfering with the development of self-responsibility in the youngster for learning to cope with their medical condition.

Dr. Miklowitz , Ph.D., has developed a therapy named Psychoeducational Family Management. As the name implies, the focus is on the education of the family with bipolar illness. He has also worked with adults, but I believe the principles of it are of enormous importance for the families of bipolar children.

I am a fan of Buckmeinster Fuller, the creative genius who gave us things like the geodesic dome. He uses the term "synergy" to describe how the combination of two elements is sometimes more than simply the sum of the parts. Dr. Miklowitz has begun to work on a therapeutic regiment that combines two approaches. By combining 25 sessions of individual interpersonal therapy with 25 sessions of family psycho-educational therapy, one in alternate weeks by separate therapists, producing 50 sessions over a one-year period, he hopes to produce a synergic, powerful treatment for bipolar illness.

These therapies may be available in your city. If not, you may need to rely on your own resources which may largely dependent on your reading books like this. Because so many children with bipolar illness have ADHD, you may find my book <u>Learning Disabilities: How to Recognize and Manage Learning and Behavioral Problems in Children</u>. It describes coping strategies for the impulsive, hyperactive youngster who has difficulty concentrating, following directions, and completing tasks.

The internet is an important source of support to all parents of bipolar children. Sites such as www. yahoo. com or www.altavista.digital.com can provide instant access to a broad range of topics dealing with this issue. Parents can join an online support group for parent of bipolar children. Once you join, they promise, "you will find yourself part of a compassionate, informed, online community of parent coping with the issues you feared were yours alone." The purpose of this particular group is "to provide quality information regarding childhood/adolescent bipolar, share experiences about our children, and assist in developing a bank of information to help parents provide the best possible atmosphere to raise and educate their bipolar children." It is well worth looking into.

A Renaissance in Anticonvulsant Medications

One of our nation's leading psychopharmacologists is Susan McElroy, M.D., of the University of Cincinnati College of Medicine. She gave an address entitled "Update on Anti-epileptic Drugs in Bipolar Disorder" at the Second International Conference of Bipolar Illness. In this talk she indicated that a number of studies in the last decade proves that a variety of anti-epileptic medications are helpful both during acute episodes of illness as well as preventing episodes and/or increasing the length of well time between episodes. These medicines may work as well as lithium and may be helpful for some patients who do not respond to lithium. Additionally, many are more easily tolerated by patients and thus patients may be more willing to stay on the medications.

Valproate (Depakote) and carbamazepine (Tegretol) are older and consequently more thoroughly studied than some of the newest anti-epileptic drugs. Gabapentine, lamotrigine and topiramate are newer; consequently, less research is available on them, but are promising for a number of reasons.

Gabapentine (Neurontine) has few side effects and there is no need to test blood levels. Lamotragine (Lamiteal) is also well tolerated by patients and may be particularly helpful to people with bipolar illness during the depressive phase. This is important because lithium is helpful for people with bipolar during the manic phase, but may be less helpful on the depressive side of the bipolar condition. Lamotrigine may also be helpful to patients who are resistant to standard mood stabilizers and antidepressants. Topirimate (Topamax) has mild to moderate side effects among them is appetite suppression. This may be helpful to those bipolar patents whose carbohydrate craving produces unhealthy weight gain.

Dr. McElroy cautioned that not every anti-epileptic medication is necessarily a mood stabilizer. Anyone medication which actually lessens the threshold for seizures (and is thus considered *pro*convulsant rather than *anti*convulsant) is one of the best anti-manic agents available. This mediation is Clozapine. The medication olanzapine (Zyprexa) also may prove to be helpful for bipolar patients. Early indications are that it is not quite as effective for difficult to treat mania as is clozapine, but is often successful.

Your computers is another source of information about medication. The quality of the information found there is always dependent of the expertise of the person or the organization who created the site. The web address of organizations such as the National Institute of Mental Health and National Depressive and Manic-Depressive organization is found at the end of this chapter. The support group for parents of bipolar kids on the internet is another place where medication is frequently discussed. If you join an online support group you are able to ask questions and share your observations about the medications prescribed for your child.

Genetics and Neurobiology

I will not attempt to thoroughly describe all the newest discoveries and the complex nature of this exciting topic. Instead, I will briefly describe some of the most interesting findings and give a short list of some of the best resources I have found.

Genetics

Dr. J. Raymond DePaulo, Jr., M.D., indicates that there is no one gene responsible for all the forms of the complex phenomena on the bipolar spectrum. It is more likely that a combination of two, three or more genes are involved in the production of most of the common forms of bipolar illness. Recent data confirm earlier studies of "linkage of manic depressive illness to loci on chromosomes 18 and to chromosome 21." Some new studies have found evidence for chromosomes besides 18 and 21.

Earlier textbooks on manic depressive illness usually focused on bipolar I illness. However, bipolar II is actually the more common genotype and may have a simpler genetic transmission. So data points to genes located on the long arm of chromosome 18 as a possible location for some of the transmission of Bipolar II illness.

Neurobiology

In the last two decades, scientists have learned more about the function of the brain than they learned in the preceding two centuries. Most of the brain researchers who have ever lived are alive right now. They have at their disposal tools such as functional magnetic resonance imaging (fMRI), a "souped-up version of the conventional MRI. It makes possible the recording of movies of the brain as it thinks, remembers, experiences emotions, and even dreams. It works by measuring faint differences in the magnetic signal between fully oxygenated blood taken from the active nerve cells, and the deoxygenated blood resulting from the extraction of oxygen by those nerve cells. The fMRI pinpoints these faint signals and, via computer enhancement, creates movies of the activated brain." (Brainscapes, p. 86)

The brain is a complex organ with interactive circuits. My attempts to learn about the fascinating new discoveries of neuroscience reminded me of a combination of chemistry and anatomy. In a nutshell, parents of bipolar children want to know what parts of the brains and what circuits produce the symptoms of mania and depression.

Among the things the hypothalamus regulates is appetite, thirst, sleep and sexual drive. The hippocampus and the amygdala are involved with memory, elation, excitement, anxiety, agitation, rage and aggression. These structures are part of the limbic system. One of the functions of the prefrontal cortex is the integration of emotional circuits. A specific region of the prefrontal cortex, the medial orbital cortex, is particularly involved in the integration of emotional information, as well as making judgements. The nucleus accumbens reinforces certain behaviors e.g., drinking, eating, and sexual activity. This nucleus is composed of dopamine containing neurons and has been identified as important for understanding addictions.

Those of us who live with people struggling with bipolar illness see this list and know these structures are likely location for manic depressive illness and the comorbid conditions of ADHD, ODD and anxiety disorder that often accompanies it.

The field of neurobiology is making much headway in understanding the circuits in the brain that affect behavior. To learn more about this you may want to read the "Causes" chapters in the books written by Demitri Papolos, M.D., and

Janice Papolos, Overcoming Depression 3rd Edition. And/or The Bipolar Child: The Definitive and Reassuring Guide to one of Childhood's Most Misunderstood Disorder. Two other resources are Brainscapes: An Introduction to What Neuroscience Has Learned About the Structure, Function, and Abilities of the Brain by Richard Restak, M.D., and Creating Mind: How the Brain Works by John Dowling

List of Important Web Sites

www.nami.org	National Alliance for the Mentally Ill
www.ndmda.org	National Depression & Manic Depression Association
www.1000deaths	1000 deaths (Suicide survivors)
www.benline.com	Benline Press (Books on Suicide and Depression)
www.afsp.org	American Foundation for Suicide Prevention
www.save.org	Suicide Awareness\Voices of Education
www.spanusa.org	Suicide Prevention Advocacy Network
www.cabf.org	Child and Adolescent Bipolar Foundation
www.bpparent.org	Bipolar Parents' Home Page
www.familiescan.org	for children with emotional & behavioral problems
www.yellowribbon.org	Yellow Ribbon Program

Suicide

Suicide is not a rare occurrence or a minor health concern. "Approximately 30,000 people of all ages kill themselves annually in the United States." ("Useful," 1986) This translates into 73 people each day. Suicide can occur when people perceive themselves as having an irresolvable life crisis.

The issue of loss is often involved. It may be the loss of one's health, the loss of loved ones, the loss of the financial means to continue a certain life style, or any other important loss. Losses are common for persons as they get older. Having a chronic, perhaps ultimately fatal illness like cancer is more likely as you get older. Your chances of seeing your close relatives and lifelong companions die is more likely in later years. People on fixed incomes may struggle to retain previous lifestyles. Historically, suicide has been highest among the elderly and lowest among the young.

SUICIDE IN THE YOUNG

Today the situation is changing. "Suicide for the elderly has somewhat declined, while the rate has soared for adolescents and young adults." ("Useful," 1986) "For adolescents, in 1950, the rate of suicide per 100,000 population was 2.7; by 1980, it had reached 8.5. This constitutes an increase of 215 percent. Suicide rates in this group appear to have increased again in the mid-1980's; by 1985, the rate per 100,000 was 10.0." (Hoberman, 1989) Furthermore, although older adolescents and young adults are more at risk for suicide than are younger adolescents and children, most recently, the suicide rate for these younger persons has risen sharply. One study indicates the "suicide rate among 10 - 14 year olds increased relatively little between 1960 and 1981; however, between 1980 and 1985, the rate for this group doubled." (Hoberman, 1989).

It always takes some time to compile the data on any condition. The Fall, 1993 issue of the Lifesavers Newsletter gave the most recent statistics on the suicide rate for the young. Dr. David Shaffer reports, "In 1991, 1,899 teenagers committed suicide and the rates (18/100,000 for boys and 3.7/100,000 for girls) are substantially the same as in 1988, when the rate for youth suicide reached an all time peak." The data also indicates that during the past 15 years, the rate of suicide for girls has remained relatively the same, whereas, the rate for boys has tripled.

The age of onset of depression has declined. Before World War II, the age of onset of a severe depressive episode typically occurred somewhere in middle age, late forties or early fifties. Since World War II, the first onset of a major depressive episode usually occurs somewhere in the late 20's or early 30's. (Gelman, 1987, p. 48).

Bipolar disturbance represents an estimated one-third of those suffering from serious depression. Bipolar illness has an early onset. The average age of onset for a first psychiatric episode for many kids with this and other forms of serious depression is 10 to 11 years old. (Hoberman, 1989, p. 9). My son was diagnosed at the Mayo Clinic as suffering from depression. Before going to Mayo he saw a local psychiatrist because I felt he clearly showed symptoms of depression. Both of these appointments occurred when Ben was eleven years old.

The possibility of suicide in a young person is frightening to all parents. Unpredictable and seemingly incomprehensible, it makes everyone feel vulnerable. I do not know how often I have heard people tell parents of a suicide victim how much they fear something like this happening in their own family. We live with the fact that 18 adolescents kill themselves in the United States every day. Suicide is the second leading cause of death for people between the ages of 15 and 24 years. (Larson, 1990, p. 1019)

CHILDREN AT RISK

In an interview for "Lifesaver Newsletter," (1993) psychiatrist Dr. Cynthia Pfeffer reports that "118 U.S. children 5 to 14 years old committed suicide in 1968, producing the very low rate of 0.3 per 100,000...By 1989, the childhood suicide rate more than doubled, and suicide advanced to the sixth leading cause of death for children in this age group." Parents and teachers want to know which children are especially at risk. Pfeffers says,

> Male children - like male adults - commit suicide more frequently than do females, and those with serious psychiatric illnesses, impaired relationships, limited adaptive skills, and extensive social problems are particularly vulnerable to future suicidal behavior. The psychiatric symptoms that especially flag suicidal children are indicators of depression: sadness, irritability, aggressive behavior, preoccupation with death, poor concentration, and withdrawal from friends and schools. Children with serious mood disorders remain at high risk later in life, and studies find that they have high rates of suicide attempts as adolescents and high rates of suicide as young adults.

ADOLESCENTS AT RISK

Dr. Garfinkel's book, Adolescent Suicide, gives a comprehensive overview of current research identifying the young people who are especially at risk of completing suicide. He cites the 1988 work by Brent, et al. who describe the psychiatric disorders of young people who completed suicide.

They found that 93 percent of the victims in the study had at least one major psychiatric diagnosis. Various types of depressive illnesses were the most common type of psychiatric disorder at the time of death. Forty one percent were diagnosed as having a severe depression disorder, 22 percent were rated as having dysthymia (mild but continuous low mood) and 7 percent were seen as experiencing a manic or hypomanic episode. Other common diagnoses at the time of death were as follows: substance abuse (41 percent); attention deficit disorder (26 percent); conduct disorder (22 percent); and anxiety disorder (15 percent) (Hoberman, 1989).

As important as these finding are, another factor emerged: co-morbidity. The existence of two or more conditions especially increases risk. Young people with serious depression *and* an anxiety disorder, particularly if they suffer from panic attacks, produce a combination that puts them at great risk. Adolescents and young adults with a serious anxiety disorder *and* alcohol/drug use are at high risk. Young schizophrenics who *also* experience the onset of a depressive episode have an elevated risk for suicide.

My son had a complex and serious depressive disorder, an anxiety disorder which included panic attacks and an attention deficit disorder. Co-morbidity is especially seen in people with bipolar illness, but not exclusively. His bipolar illness co-morbid with anxiety disorder and ADD makes him an appropriate example of a typical young person at elevated risk for completing suicide. Was substance abuse an issue for him? His single but unusual drinking incident makes me wonder if he did not have the potential for developing a problem in this area. If he had, he would have been like so many others who use it to self-medicate the anxiety so frequently associated with depression.

ATTEMPTERS VS COMPLETERS

Historically, there are two factors distinguishing people who attempt suicide as compared to those who complete suicide. First is the type of condition they suffered. Attempters were described as having neurosis or personality disorders rather than combinations of depression, anxiety, substance abuse, or schizophrenia.

The other factor found between attempters and completers is a gender difference. Females attempt suicide four times as often as do males ("Useful," 1986), but more men are likely to complete suicide than are females. "Males account for three-fourths of all committed suicide." ("Useful," 1986). Youthful suicide is particularly dominated by males; the rate is nearly five times that of females. Furthermore, the rate of suicide between 1950 and 1980 has increased 295 percent for males, whereas the rate for females has only increased by 67 percent (Hoberman, 1989).

In recent years, a third factor has emerged -- the availability of a lethal weapon. The presence of a gun in the home elevates risk, especially for adolescents and young adults. Brent and Perper note that from 1933 (the Great Depression) to 1982 the rate of suicide in the United States for 10 - 24 year olds increased 1.3 fold while the rate in firearms suicide for that group rose 2.4 fold. They further report that suicide rates are lower in those parts of the country where fewer people own guns.

It is important to remember that typically 15 percent of people suffering from serious co-morbid conditions (depression, anxiety, drug/alcohol abuse and schizophrenia) will use whatever means is available to end their lives. However, the presence of an easily available firearm may, on the other hand, increase the risk that an uninhibited, impulsive young person without a serious psychiatric disorder will act on a sudden suicidal impulse.

When thinking about the difference between attempters and completers, it is a mistake to think a person who has a history of attempts will never complete it. Information from the Department of Health tells us: "People who have made serious suicide attempts are at highest risk for actually killing themselves. The suicide rate for repeat attempters is up to 643 times higher than the overall rate in the general population. Between 20 - 50 percent of the people who commit suicide had previously made attempts." ("Useful," 1986)

The increase in suicide among young people may be resulting from the combination of earlier onset of depressive illness, the increased rate of depression at this particular time in history, and an increase in ownership of guns.

WHAT ARE YOUNG ATTEMPTERS OR COMPLETERS TRYING TO DO?

You might think the answer to the question is obvious. The suicidal person wants to die. But this may not be true for many adolescents. "In a recent study of Minnesota teenagers, 64 percent of suicide attempters said they really did not want to die".

("Supporting," 1986). In fact, "Follow-up studies (of persons who attempted but did not complete suicide) reveal their intense ambivalence about dying. Not only are they glad to be alive, but for many, a suicide attempt marked a turning point. It was a dramatic signal that their problems demanded serious and immediate attention. Most of those who survived their suicide attempts indicated that what they really wanted was a change in their lives ("Useful," 1986).

That to me is the key; they wanted a change in their lives. Joseph Campbell (1990) gives us some insight into this. He says,

> The New Testament teaches dying to one's self, literally suffering the pain of death to the world and its values. This is the vocabulary of the mystics. Now, suicide is also a symbolic act. It casts off the psychological posture that you happen to be in at the time, so that you may come into a better one. You die to your current life in order to come to another of some kind. But, as Jung says, you'd better not get caught in a symbolic situation. You don't have to die, really, physically. All you have to do is die spiritually and be reborn to a larger way of living.

You do not have to literally die to change your life. When I say that what my son did was stupid, I mean Ben took an idea that is symbolically true and acted it out literally. Or as the famous psychiatrist Carl Jung might have said, the best way to die to one way of life and to be born to a new, larger way of life is to change your attitude.

Committing suicide is an especially powerful idea in the mind of many adolescents. Evidence for this is found in the statistics on suicide attempters. When the data from all age groups are compared, there are approximately ten attempts for every one completed suicide. But when you look at attempts versus completions for young people, "the ratio for youth is 25 - 50 suicide attempts for every one suicide completion" ("Useful, " 1986).

Suicide is a symbolic act which speaks to the psychological issue for young people in their particular stage of life. Adolescence is a time of putting aside one way of life, i.e., childhood, and being re-born into a new way of life, i.e., adulthood. The theme of transition is a strong force in the adolescents' minds and it is easy to see how they may physically act out their psychological process. It is lucky for all of us that there are 25 - 50 attempts for every completed suicide. These young people have a chance to see that the goal was change rather than death.

PREVENTION PROGRAMS
OF THE PAST

"Several studies have demonstrated that suicide prevention programs have not made a significant impact on the rate of suicides." In recent years, a number of suicide prevention curricula have been developed specifically targeted to youth. Dr. Garfinkel notes the curricula of these programs tend to focus on the circumstances surrounding suicides (Hoberman, 1989, pp. 22-23). This is not effective because "suicide victims kill themselves when confronted with typical stress situations that most of us face without major difficulty. Stressors alone do not likely pose a risk for the adolescent. Instead, it appears to be the existence of stressors for particular individuals with pre-existing psychiatric conditions that create a climate of risk."

In my son's case, the stressor may have been his pile of unfinished school work. He was given exactly the same assignments everyone else got. The difficulty arose from his own inability to finish the work the rest of the class managed to complete on time. Procrastination is a common characteristic of persons with depressive illness. This, plus the cognitive difficulties associated with his depression, ADHD, and anxiety all contributed to create the pile of unfinished work.

Rather than being a logical act growing out of an impossible life situation, adolescent suicide is often an impulsive act. Garfinkel puts it this way: "The seemingly impulsive, crisis-nature of the actual suicide is impressive. Relatively few suicides showed evidence of advance planning or even precautions against being stopped or discovered at the time of the act." (Hoberman, 1989, p. 17)

WARNING SIGNS

Suicide prevention in the past has often focused on looking for warning signs. These signs include:

(1) Previous Suicide attempts
People who have made serious suicide attempts are at high risk for actually killing themselves.

(2) Suicide talk
People who commit suicide often talk about it first. Statements like, "They'd be better off without me," or "No one will have to worry about me much longer," can be give-aways. A more offhand "I've had it," may also be a clue.

(3) Making arrangements
Some suicidal individuals take steps to put their affairs in order. They draw up or alter their wills, give away prized possessions, make arrangements for pets, or otherwise act as if they are preparing for a trip. They talk vaguely about going away.

(4) Personality or Behavior Change
A normally buoyant person may seem increasingly down for no apparent reason. There may be a loss of interest in school, work, friends, hobbies, and recreational activities that gave them pleasure in the past. They may begin to express a sense of worthlessness or hopelessness, or excessive guilt.

(5) Clinical Depression
While 85 percent of depressed people are not suicidal, most of the suicide-prone are depressed. ("Useful," 1986, pp. 15-16)

The Use of Warning Signs

The question is: Although these signs are frequently present before a suicide, are they easily detected by others in the environment? To answer this, I think about my son's death. Any previous attempts Ben may have made were not done in a manner that I recognized as warnings. He did tell his therapist early in treatment that he had pointed a gun at his head. When she told me this, it was news to me. He probably fooled around dangerously with guns but never did this when adults were around. Ben's accident-prone behavior throughout his life seems now to be an ongoing flirtation with danger.

His suicide talk consisted of the remark, "A lot you'd care if something happened to me." This statement was made in the context of our conversation about his over-eating. I did not catch it as suicidal talk. Did he put affairs in order? He had cleaned his room the week before, but in preparation for a guest. We saw behavioral change, but this was expected with the change in medication he was undergoing. We thought his clinical depression had lifted and hoped his therapy could be reduced. He had been looking forward to things such as going to horse shows with his riding instructor and using the new saddle we just bought for his daily horseback riding.

When a surviving family member looks back on the last days of the life of a person who commits suicide, it is possible to pick up some clues. But at the time they are happening, these behaviors are not blatantly different from what is happening in the person's life on any other day. Someone once said that if President Kennedy had not been shot, no one would remember he was in Dallas in November of 1963. Likewise, if my son had not died I would not be able to recall what happened the last week in May, 1989.

Dr. Garfinkel cautions against an over-emphasis on precipitating events, the presence of stressors, or signs of plans to die. The impulsive nature of suicide in young people makes preventing particular suicides unlikely (Hoberman, 1989). What I have learned in the last few years leads me to agree with that assertion. People I have met in suicide survivors' support groups indicate there were few, if any, distinct indications their loved ones were contemplating suicide. These people are loving, bright individuals. Most of them, like myself, did not have a clue their loved one was at risk of committing suicide. The victim did not *clearly* display many of the warning signs of suicide, nor did their behavior seem dramatically different on the day it occurred or in the weeks preceding the death.

Asking adults to be alert to signs and making them responsible for prevention places an unrealistic and consequently unfair burden on them. Research indicates "There is no profile or checklist for identifying a suicidal person. Suicide, like much of human behavior, is difficult to predict. Despite their best efforts, even experts cannot say whether or when a person will try to commit suicide" ("Useful," 1986).

An over-emphasis on the stressors immediately preceding a person's death not only prevents us from having a clear understanding of the cause of the problem, which is the psychiatric illness, but when we overemphasize the preceding stressor it may cause the survivors to torture themselves unnecessarily.

After a suicide, survivors often say, "If only I had done this or if I had done that the suicide may have been prevented." The person's suicide may have had little to do with the individual's outer life situation. Recent work comparing the lives of those who kill themselves, those who attempted, and those who died of natural causes reveals that, in the main, the lives of those who kill themselves are often no worse than those of others who carry on. To the objective outsider, their situations are far from hopeless, and there are ways other than suicide to solve their problems. ("Useful," 1986) It is not so much the circumstances of a person's life, but the pain of their illness which is relevant.

Rather than trying to prevent suicide by looking for warning signs or focusing on the preceding stressor or trigger, it seems more logical to focus on the cause, namely the psychiatric conditions. Emphasizing the diagnosis and treatment of depression, anxiety disorder, and drug/alcohol abuse makes sense. These are very common and treatable disorders.

It may seem paradoxical for me to advocate the importance of diagnosis and treatment of these conditions since my own child completed suicide while seeing a therapist on a regular basis. Research does, however, indicate treatment as a factor helpful in reducing risk. We sought the best treatment program available in our region. I feel strongly that Ben's therapist is one of the finest adolescent psychiatrists in our state. She had excellent rapport with him. Ben always reported feeling so much better after seeing her, and we felt there were many results from each of their sessions. We were extremely lucky to have found an adolescent psychiatrist as knowledgeable as she was in the current research in mood disorder, and one who specialized in working with children and adolescents with this condition. Garry and I did not mind driving three hours to her office in another city and three hours back home again to get this level of care for our son. I do not blame my son's death on his therapist for not predicting when he would be suicidal. Suicide is an impulsive act. How is anyone going to predict when an impulsive act is going to occur?

Getting medical treatment for any illness does not necessarily mean the doctor is going to be able to "fix" the condition. If my son had cancer, no one would assume that getting medical treatment for his condition would guarantee survival. Bipolar illness, like cancer, is a very serious condition. For everyone who has the illness, it is a condition which requires a significant amount of care and monitoring. Historically, for approximately

20 percent of people with bipolar illness, the condition is fatal. Depression may be the common cold of psychiatry, but the difference between depression and a cold is that depression can kill you.

Depression in young persons has generally been undiagnosed and untreated. Although I recognize suicide has been with us throughout history and probably always will be, a more realistic goal is to increase the percentage of persons with depression receiving proper treatment for the condition. Although the number of adults seeking treatment for depression has improved in recent years, children and adolescents do not yet have the same level of care as is currently received by adults. Too many young people with mild to severe depression are suffering unnecessarily.

THE NEED FOR SCREENING

Teachers and health care professionals want to help prevent suicide in the young when possible. Unfortunately, studies indicate that teachers are in the same situation as parents. They also cannot easily detect the presence of depression in children or adolescents. Physicians likewise often do not identify depression in patients who complete suicide. "One study found that half to three-quarters of nonpsychiatrist medical doctors miss it." (Gelman, 1987) This finding indicates a need for the use of a screening device. Before outlining the use of screening, the following comments are important.

Although teachers can be helpful in identifying depression in children and adolescents, it may be unwise to mandate that they be held accountable for doing this. Past experience with government bureaucracy in enforcing accountability is as follows: If teachers are held responsible for identifying depression in their students

rules and regulations will be promulgated

more paper work will be added to the work load of these already overburdened people, and

when a student, impulsively and without clear signs of distress, does commit suicide there may be efforts to produce blame.

I think the last thing anyone wants to do is increase blame and guilt adults may feel when a youngster dies. Teachers are not trained to spot depressive illness, and it's unfair to make them responsible.

I would like to suggest that this challenging health issue be handled like any other health problem: by a combination of professional persons and volunteer initial screening. Schools do routine visual and audiotory screening in elementary school. The screening for depression in young people could be done very easily, and I believe it is very important to do.

What I am suggesting is something a few school systems are already doing. They give a simple paper and pencil test to their older students. It would consist of having the pupils rate themselves (Most of the time, Sometimes, or Never) on statements such as these:

I sleep very well.
I feel like crying.
I get stomach aches.

I think life isn't worth living.
I am good at things I do.
I am easily cheered up.
I have lots of energy.
I feel very lonely.
I feel very bored.
I have horrible dreams.

You will note that the creator of this screening tool worded some of the items positively and others negatively. This was done deliberately to avoid bias. This screening tool can be handed out by the teacher to the class. (The entire screening tool is found in the appendix of this book.) Because youngsters often experience the symptoms of depression more strongly toward the end of the day rather than the beginning, it may be wise to distribute this screening device during the last 15 minutes of the school day rather than first thing in the morning.

Children with bipolar illness need to be screened for the manic side of their condition as well as the depressive. Again I believe that teachers can be very helpful, but I do not wish to put an excessive burden on their already busy schedules. We know that many children with bipolar illness have the symptoms of ADHD; in fact they often have more symptoms of ADHD than do children who simply have ADHD and aren't bipolar. In the last decade teachers have become alert to ADHD, thus the logical screening for teachers to use may be the list of symptoms of ADHD. One can simply count the number of symptoms the child has. If the number is small, the child may simply have ADHD. But if the child has a large number of symptoms, the student should be referred to a professional for further evaluation for possible bipolar illness.

In making the comparison between sensory screening and depression screening, I hope that I will not be misunderstood. I commend the wonderful volunteers who unselfishly give of their time to do the important work of vision and hearing screening each year. But I would like to continue with this comparison between sensory screening and a possible screening for depression to make the point that, in my opinion, screening for depression has a greater priority. I hope you will forgive me if, as a bereaved parent, I state the case fairly strongly.

"In 1980 3,442 persons aged 15 - 19 committed suicide" (Hoberman, 1989). Did three or four thousand school aged youngster die in 1980 because they were slightly near-sighted or far-sighted? I am not aware of an alarming increased rate of hearing problems in this country. In contrast, the age of onset of depression seems to be occurring younger now than in years past. remember that in 1986, 39 percent of adolescents reported suffering from some level of depression. There is also a dramatic increase in the suicide rate for adolescents.

Hearing and vision screening is done because these problems could interfere with learning. Does not the "diminished ability to think or concentrate," "slowed thinking or indecisiveness," "loss of interest or pleasure in usual activities," "fatigue or loss of energy," "change in sleeping patterns," and the "feelings of worthlessness" that are associated with depression and which translate into the "decline in the quality of school work" also interfere with learning? Does not depressive illness interfere with learning just as much as problems with vision or hearing?

"Each year in the United States, approximately 5,000 young people age 24 and younger commit suicide ("Teen," 1985). We are not dealing with rare phenomena but with a significant public health problem which research indicates is generally undertreated.

The National Institute of Mental Health reports that undiagnosed and untreated, "Youngsters with this problem are left to their own resources in dealing with their illness. These young people often rely on passive or negative behaviors in their attempts to deal with problems" ("Adolescent," 1986). My son did not have a behavior problem in school, but he, like many other depressed kids, was passive. How many depressed youth develop behavior problems and are treated as "bad" rather than youngsters with an undiagnosed illness?

When the results of screening indicate the presence of depression, the students can be treated like anyone else with a medical problem. It is not the parents' fault when a youngster needs glasses to correct his vision. Why would we assume it is the parents' fault when a youngster needs treatment for depression?

A NO-BLAME APPROACH

General education about depression as a biological condition can be helpful, and it would decrease the blame associated with the condition. Many other illnesses used to have shame associated with them. Years ago, cancer was seen as something of which to be ashamed. In the past, attempts were made to hide the fact that a person had the disease; sometimes it was covered up as the cause of death on the death certificate. Today there is not any stigma of blame associated with cancer. We only think of persons with cancer as innocent victims of a cruel disease.

I feel it would be a positive step forward if the same could be done for depressive illness. I think all too often when family members hear that their loved one is depressed, it translates in their mind as: "What have I done to cause the problem?" Frequently, the environment had little to do with the illness.

Sitting in my suicide support group has been a real eye-opening experience for me. I look at the wonderful people sitting in that room with me, and it becomes perfectly clear these people have nothing to feel guilty about. This has helped me to put a measure of reality into my own situation. I could choose to be hard on myself and find ways to feel guilty about Ben's death. I would, however, never be that unobjective about other people. Seeing the contrast between how I could choose to think about my own situation and how I actually see other people, I have come to see that I too have no logical reason to feel guilty about his depression or his death.

It would be wonderful if other people when hearing the words, "your loved one may have a problem with depression" would not feel that it is somehow their fault. I think the most helpful way to do this is to stress the biochemical theories of depression. Getting scientific information helps us becoming objective.

IS REDUCTION OF THE SUICIDE RATE AN ATTAINABLE GOAL?

I do not know if we can reduce the number of suicides. I do not think it is wise to make it a goal. Not all suicides are preventable. Suicide is too complicated an issue to have one simple answer. A historical and worldwide perspective on suicide is useful.

Suicide is as old as it is universal. People have been killing themselves since the beginning of recorded time. Suicide has meant different things among various cultures through the ages. It has not always evoked horror. It is mentioned matter-of-factly in the Bible. It was tolerated, even honored, as a particularly decent death in ancient Greece and Rome. Suicide continues to be so honored in Asian and Middle Eastern societies today. It was the means to heaven for early Christian martyrs and is now believed by Islamic martyrs to be their ticket to salvation. Suicide has meant delivery from military defeat and escape from enslavement.

Suicide survived religious and secular transformation in the sixth century, as a sin against God and a crime against the community, to become a major theme for Renaissance writers. It was a cause for enlightenment philosophers and a fashion among melancholy nineteenth century romantics. In the last century, suicide captured the interest of mental health scientists, and the modern study of suicide got under way. What has been defended as an intellectual choice by enlightenment thinkers came to be seen as, if not a sign of mental illness, a means of relief from psychic pain and sorrow ("Useful," 1986).

Because it is unlikely that we have yet come to the final chapter in our discoveries about suicide, perhaps it is unwise to make any statement about the ability to reduce suicide. What is clear, however, is that we now have effective means of treating depression and that we have a large number of people who are not receiving it. Of the estimated 25 - 35 million people with severe depression, at least fifty percent are not getting treatment.

Since at least 80 percent of severely depressed persons and probably nearly all of those with mild cases could be significantly helped with presently available methods of treatment, an aggressive approach to identification and treatment of depression seems to be a realistic goal. Maybe if we focused on that, the suicide rate would take care of itself. Even if it was not reduced, we as a nation may feel we did our best to deal with one of suicide's major causes. We would have helped to decrease the unnecessary suffering in our young people, the one group that has not had an increase in health care in the last 30 years.

To hear the phrase "suicide is preventable" is analogous to hearing that "cancer is curable." It may be more precise to say: Some types of cancer may be cured if detected early, if patients receive competent medical treatment, and if they are determined to survive. A sense of hope for the future is an important ingredient. Similarly, some people with depressive illness, anxiety disorder, schizophrenia, and those with some major traumatic loss or serious physical illness may be deterred from completing suicide if detected early and the patients receive competent medical treatment and finds within themselves an attitude of determination to survive. A sense of hope for the future is an important ingredient for them as well.

When thinking about death, we come back to a paradox. What my son did was an impulsive act, and his therapist quite correctly called it stupid. My son is not to be admired for his act, but for some mysterious reason I can not help but believe it was his fate. I always come back to the message I received as I stood over Ben's body: "This was supposed to happen this day."

WHEN EVERYTHING YOU'VE TRIED FEELS LIKE FAILURE

This book outlined an elective class designed to work with young people with depression and anxiety. Research indicates it has a good chance of working. This class should give hope to the many parents who struggle with children with emotional difficulties. By combining current advances in medicine with effective teaching, there is hope we can help the many young people who need it.

The success of the program for any given student will depend on how serious their emotional problems are and how multifaceted they are. Ben had three serious disorders. Helping him to cope with that combination of problems was extremely difficult. Helping any young person learn to cope with challenges is always difficult. Luckily, most cases of depression are unipolar and are not associated with a learning disability.

During my years as a college instructor, I taught a class entitled "The Psychology of the Exceptional Child." Each year I required the class to compare the various ways of working with exceptionally capable students. My students were also required to compare the techniques used to work with children who have problems with school. What they discovered is that almost anything done with capable youngsters works fairly well. Having gifted students skip a grade, or placing gifted students in special classrooms, or keeping them in their regular grade but giving them enrichment assignments can be successful for gifted students. Occasionally, even doing little if anything for them still works, because exceptionally capable youngsters often find ways of making good use of their time on their own. They will read or engage themselves in a hobby that teaches them useful things. Although no generalization is true for every child, most of the time whatever is done for gifted students is successful.

When my students analyzed strategies for working with children who have learning problems, they found a different picture. Putting these students in separate classrooms isolates them, preventing them from benefiting from the interaction they would get from capable classmates who can serve as role models. In an isolated situation, teachers may begin to expect less from them, and they in turn may begin to expect less of themselves. But if they are left in a classroom with no special help, they find it difficult to handle. If their learning problems are not understood, they do not feel comfortable. Repeating a grade usually does not benefit a child with learning problems.

Almost any method used with especially capable students has a good chance of working; whereas, no method of working with students with difficulties will necessarily guarantee success. We need to recognize that working with difficult kids is just plain hard work. And, no matter how hard we try to help these students, we may not succeed.

The methods we use need to match the problems they have. When I look back on Ben's life, I see how many of the things I did for Ben did not match his problem. Often I would advise him to concentrate harder. Continually asking a child with an attention deficit to concentrate is ridiculous. The inability to concentrate is the major characteristic of the condition. I also frequently told him to think about the consequences of his behavior before he acted. Impulsively is the second major characteristic of attention deficit. ADHD is a deficit of thinking, i.e., inability to concentrate and a lack of ability to plan.

On the other hand, some of the things I did to help Ben were exactly the right thing to do to meet his needs. Even this had limited success because of the seriousness of his condition. This book's many suggestions to help the parents and teachers of students with difficulties should not inadvertently become a weapon used to blame anyone when things do not work out well for the young person. When a student commits suicide, often the parents will say, "If only I had done this or that, things might have been different; we might have prevented the death." Even when things are done to help a student, it does not necessary follow that all of their problems will be solved.

It is important to have a balanced perspective on the techniques used to help young people with problems. It is not logical (or fair) to blame the youngster when things do not work out as we hoped. It is equally unfair to blame ourselves -- the parents, the teacher, the doctors who tried their best to help them. When I was crying after Ben's death and asking myself, "Wasn't there any way we could have saved him?", I concluded that if Ben's problems would have been easy, we probably would have been able to help him find a way. This also gave me a glimpse into Ben's thinking. He had been through many strategies and perhaps he concluded that nothing would ever work out for him.

The good news for most parents is that the vast majority of young people with emotional problems do not have a condition as complex or serious as Ben's. An analogy to vision problems is useful here. Some people are blessed with perfect vision, but it is very common for people to have a mild problem. A pair of glasses or contact lenses are usually enough to give the needed correction. Similarly, while most people never experience depression or anxiety disorder, perhaps as many as 40 percent of the adolescent population do have at least a mild form of depression often with concurrent anxiety. Some experience anxiety alone. At least 80 percent would be significantly helped by the cognitive and social skills training for their depression. Anxiety is treated with various coping strategies. Research tells us that these methods, with the use of medication when appropriate, can provide help to young people who need it.

For young people who are blind, glasses are ineffective. It is unfair to blame students with very serious vision impairments because they cannot see and because they do not respond favorably to a pair of glasses. Neither is it logical to say that glasses, in general, do not work simply because they are incapable of making the blind see. It is neither the doctor's fault nor the eye glass company's fault for failing to cure the blindness.

Similarly, there is a percentage of young people with severe or complex depressions. It is not their fault they do not respond favorably to the treatment programs that succeed in helping the majority who suffer from depression. Neither is it logical to say that cognitive and social skills training for depression and techniques to cope with anxiety are not effective because some youngsters still take their own lives even after participating in these kinds of programs. It is unfair to blame psychiatrists who undoubtedly suffer enormously when some of their patients choose suicide.

Paradoxically, although medication relieves the symptoms of depression for most people who take them, it is not clear that they curb the rate of suicide. Antidepressants were first developed in the mid 1950's. The rate of suicide has not decreased since they became available. Antidepressants are not at fault for failing to cure all people with depression, nor are they to blame for the increased rate of suicide among young people. We live in an Age of Depression.

No one is to blame. We all did the best we can. The challenge is to do what is possible -- effectively treat those cases that can be helped.

One last analogy describes my understanding of what Ben faced in his struggle with three conditions. Helen Keller was born with two problems: she was blind and deaf. We can imagine what it would be like to become blind by putting something over our eyes. We attempt to understand deafness by blocking our ears, although this is harder to do. Living one day with those two conditions would give someone a small glimpse of what life is like with those handicaps. Even then, our appreciation for overcoming these problems is limited, because Keller was born with these conditions and had to acquire language without benefit of hearing the spoken word - an extremely difficult task.

When a child is born with three different problems: depression (distorted thinking), anxiety disorder (pervasive fearfulness), and ADHD (deficient thinking), the problems may be as difficult to deal with as were Keller's dual disabilities. It was hard for the adults in Ben's life to understand the problems he faced. It is especially incomprehensible for us when a child like Ben is intelligent, lives in a comfortable home, and attends a school with competent teachers. Keller's problems were difficult, but at least they were obvious. Children with depression, anxiety, and

ADHD are a problem for themselves and for their parents, teachers, and peers. The cause of their problems is not obvious.

As a child, Keller did finally get the specialized help that allowed her to overcome her disabilities. Finger spelling and Braille are useful tools. But if she had not been extraordinarily bright, she may not have been able to develop the potential she had. Work with young people with emotional problems must also focus on building competencies. As we build these competencies we will succeed in saving many young people who might not otherwise have been saved. In the work of helping young people with depression, anxiety, and ADHD, we may be guided by the Serenity Prayer: God grant me the serenity to accept the things I cannot change, the courage to change the things I can, and the wisdom to know the difference.

Programs like cognitive therapy, social skills training, and those methods used to cope with anxiety have great potential to help young people today. What is needed is the determination to make successful programs available to any student who chooses to have them. For students like Ben, whose conditions are severe and complex, the program may not completely solve the problem. It will, however, reduce some of the pain they suffer.

Ben's words, "You do not know what it means to me to have someone who understands," should never be forgotten.

Contents - Appendix 1

I. Screening instrument for Fourth - Sixth Grade.

II Recommended curriculum for 7th - 12th Grade

A. For Parents, Teachers, and Health Professionals

Psychiatric disorders of almost all suicide completers
Differences between suicide attempters and completers
Stressors preceding most adolescent suicide attempts
Symptom changes
Conditions commonly accompanying depression
How adolescents can help one another
Self-help for depressed youth

B. Especially for Health Professionals

Recommendations to the media -   Things to Avoid
Seasonal variations on suicide rates
General treatment goals for depressed youth
Crisis intervention for depressed persons
Modified hypoglycemic diet for persons on lithium

Note: Some of this material was obtained from a workshop presented by Dr. H. Hoberman on adolescent suicide.

I Instrument for Fourth - Sixth Grade

	Most of the time	Sometimes	Never
I look forward to things as much as I used to			
I sleep very well			
I feel like crying			
I like to go out to play			
I feel like running away			
I get stomach aches			
I have lots of energy			
I enjoy my food			
I can stick up for myself			
I think life isn't worth living			
I am good at things I do			
I enjoy the things I do as much as I used to			
I like talking with my family			
I have horrible dreams			
I feel very lonely			
I am easily cheered up			
I feel so sad I can hardly stand it			
I feel very bored			

Request for reprints to Dr. P. Birleson, The Young People's Unit, Tipperline House, Tipperline Road, Edinburgh EH105HF, U.K.

This is an instrument developed in 1980 when the validity of depressive disorders in childhood was not yet appreciated and when there was no self-rating scale available for children. The author used the term "depressive disorder" to refer to depression that is serious enough to impair a person's ability to function for a period of time, usually at least a number of weeks. This would exclude temporary grief reactions, normal moods shifts, demoralization, and the presence of ongoing personality traits.

The author wrote that demoralization is different from pure depression disorder in that it is not as pervasive. Children who are demoralized can still enjoy themselves some of the time, sleep normally, and do not experience unusual appetite. Although they too may develop a sense of hopelessness and show signs of sadness, demoralization is often seen as either secondary to other psychiatric conditions or as a normal reaction to failure.

The depression scale for children was tested by comparing data from various groups of children.

A. Youngsters who were referred to the department of child psychiatry in a hospital because of clinical depression

B. Two sets of youngsters who had psychological/behavioral problems but were not diagnosed as suffering primarily from depression

C. Youngsters from a local elementary school

This self-rating instrument, by definition, does not need to be given by a psychiatrist. Because it is in the public domain, its use is not restricted. It can easily be given to any child or group of children. Because many youngsters experience depression around 4th grade, the best strategy would be to start screening then. Twice a year, mid-September and mid-March, would be best because of the seasonal effect light has on depression. A simple record of the results should be kept to help health care worker see a historical pattern in the youngsters condition.

To my knowledge there are no guidelines that differentiate the various levels of depression by specific ranges in the scores cited in the study done on this test. The author did find that none of the youngsters from the local elementary school scored over 11. An examination of the data from the groups indicate that a score of 13 or above is likely to be reasonably indicative of "depressive disorder," although there may be an acceptable false positive or false negative of less than 20%.

Note that some of the symptoms of depression are stated in the positive form; e.g., "I feel very lonely." Other symptoms are stated in their negative form; e.g., "I am easily cheered up." This was done to avoid bias. Unfortunately, this also complicates the scoring process. To allow children to also score it themselves, a revised format of this screening tool is now being developed. It is available by sending a self addressed stamped envelope to Benline Press or by visiting the web site www.benline.com or the web site of CABF www.cabf.com.

It may be prudent to suggest that youngsters with very low scores do not experience any level of depression, and children whose scores approach 10 may suffer from mild or moderate depression. Since the ability to concentrate and remember is affected by depression, even milder forms of depression interfere with their ability to do well academically. Thus, these milder forms of depression deserve some attention. Certainly any child whose score is 11 or above should be referred to health care professionals for further assessment.

II. Recommended Curriculum for 7th - 12th Grade

Dr. David Burns' *Ten Days To Self-Esteem* contains an easy to use depression checklist and an anxiety inventory. The scoring is easily accomplished, enabling students to see for themselves how they are doing. Burns provides a scoring key for the various levels of depression and anxiety. In the 1993 edition, a score of 0 - 4 = no depression, 5 - 10 = normal but unhappy, 11 - 20 = mild depression, 21 - 30 = moderate, 31 - 45 = severe.

Burns' text was designed as a workbook to help people who suffer from depression and anxiety. Pioneered and tested at the Presbyterian Medical Center at Philadelphia, careful research establishes its effectiveness. A leaders manual is also available, enabling classroom teachers who are willing to master this curriculum to use cognitive techniques efficiently with groups.

In the next few years I intend to publish a book entitled *Suicide Prevention: Can It Be Done?*-- a natural extension of the workshop I now present using the same title. It examines all of the factors top researchers in the field have identified as putting someone at high risk for suicide.

The content of that unpublished work is more inclusive than the chapters here that focus primarily on depression and anxiety. The new book has specific chapters on learning disabilities (especially ADHD), alcohol and drug abuse, and personality disorders (especially borderline personality and antisocial personality). It is my belief that ultimately these factors need to included in an elective class for grade 7 - 12. However, since depression and anxiety remain the single most important risk factors, the workbook *Ten Days To Self-Esteem* and the material covered here in *Depression in the Young* give a genuinely useful working foundation that will help the majority of youngsters.

A.1 PSYCHIATRIC DISORDER

Almost all suicide completers have a psychiatric disorder.

Depressive disorder

  Bipolar disorder

  Alcohol or drug abuse

  Antisocial behavior

  Attention Deficit-Hyperactivity Disorder

A.2 DIFFERENCES BETWEEN ADOLESCENT SUICIDE ATTEMPTERS AND COMPLETERS

  Gender

    More females attempt than do males
    (ratio of at least 10 to 1)

    More males complete than do females
    (ratio of approximately 5 to 1)

2.   Availability of firearms

Suicide completion is at least four times more likely in a home in which firearms are accessible.

A.3 STRESSORS

Attempters have two times as many negative life events in the last six months: a greater number of negative life events in their lifetime.

Breakup with boy/girlfriend

Trouble with sibling

Change in family financial status

Parents' divorce

Losing close friend

Trouble with teacher

Change to a new school

Personal illness or injury

Failing grades

Increased arguments with parents

Stressors: Loss and conflict

A.4 SYMPTOMS CHANGE AS DEPRESSED CHILDREN REACH ADOLESCENCE AND YOUNG ADULTHOOD

A. Symptoms that decrease with age

Depressed appearance

Self-esteem problems

Somatic complaints

Hallucinations

B. Symptoms that remain stable with age

Depressed mood

Poor concentration

Insomnia

Suicidal thoughts and attempts

C. Symptoms that increase with age

Anhedonia - (inability to experience pleasure)

Diurnal mood - (feeling worse in morning than later in the day)

Hopelessness

Psychomotor retardation - slowed speech

Definitive delusions - illogical assumptions about oneself
or others

A.5   LIST OF CONDITIONS COMMONLY ACCOMPANYING DEPRESSION

Only 25% of children and adolescents have depression alone. 75% have at least one other (co-morbid) condition

A. External Disorder - problems easily seen by and bothersome to other people.

ADHD (inattention, impulsive, overactive)

Conduct Disorder (cannot follow rules at home or at school)

Learning Disabilities (Dyslexia - cannot read, spell or learn a foreign language; dyscalcula - cannot do math)

Delinquency - involvement with law enforcement

B. Internal Disorders - Problems that are internally painful to the person, but not necessarily troublesome to others

Anxiety Disorder - shortness of breath, dizziness, a sinking feeling in the stomach, and rapid heartbeat

Eating Disorder - anorexia, bulimia, obesity

Substance Abuse - the beginnings of alcoholism and/or drug addiction

A.6 HOW ADOLESCENTS CAN HELP ONE ANOTHER

Care about your friends; be available and listen

Explore possible solutions to problems, but don't tell friends what to do.

Try to understand without judging, arguing, denying, or minimizing feelings.

Tolerate depressed, irritable moods

Help to remember good things about them and their life.

Emphasize that they can live through deep hurt and that there are people who care.

Explore what things they can look forward to.

Reach out to fringe kids.

Maintain confidence, but if really worried about suicide, don't take chance - alert responsible adult.

A.7   SELF-HELP FOR DEPRESSED YOUTH

Try to understand if particular things are making you
   depressed.

Tell someone you trust how you feel - express yourself
   and get feelings out.

If necessary, write out feelings.

Be with other people, even if hard; avoid being alone.

Exercise - be physically active.

Do at least one thing your really enjoy, even if you don't
   want to do it.

Find something you did well or were satisfied with and
   praise yourself

Look your best.

Get out of the house and do something.

A.9 POSSIBLE SIGNS OF DISTRESSED YOUTH OUT OF CLASSROOM

Overhearing remarks indicative of significant unhappiness or despair.

Knowledge that prized possessions are being given away.

Loss of interest in extracurricular activities.

Direct suicide threats or attempts.

Marked emotionality.

Recent depression to suicidal behavior in family.

Recent conflict or losses in close relationships.

Increased and heavy use of alcohol or drugs

B. 1   GUIDELINES FOR TEACHERS IN DEALING WITH SUICIDAL COMMUNICATION

1. *Avoid* oversimplifying the many factors that cause the suicide

2. *Avoid* sensationalizing the suicide

3. *Avoid* glorifying the victim

4. *Avoid* making the suicide appear to be a rewarding experience or an appropriate or effective tool to achieve a personal gain

5. *Avoid* depicting the method of the suicide

6. *Avoid* emphasis to stressor or simplistic psychological presses as much as pressures

7 *Avoid* massive or repeated doses of press coverage

B 2 SEASONAL VARIATIONS ON SUICIDE RATES
Effect of light on persons with depressive illness

People who have bipolar I or major depression (typical pattern) along with impulsive/aggressive behavior are affected by rate of change in the ratio of light VS darkness. The times when change is fastest is during the spring and fall.

People who have bipolar II and others with the atypical pattern are effected by the amount of light. Summer daylight is twice as long as winter daylight. Atypical clients often have winter depression and summer hypomania. They are especially at risk during switch from depression into hypomania.

Spring has higher rate of suicide. October also shows elevated risk but not as high as March - June.

Monthly Peak Occurrences of Suicide
a review based on 61 studies (Number indicate data points)

Jan 1
Feb 1
Mar 7
April 11
May 20
June 8
July 1
Aug 1
Sep 0.5
Oct 6
Nov 3
Dec 4

B.3   GENERAL TREATMENT GOALS FOR DEPRESSED YOUTH

1. Manage immediate stressors.

2. Manage depressive symptoms.

3. Manage symptoms of co-morbid disorders.

4. Reduce impairing depressive symptoms.

5. Reduce chronic stressors, including family dysfunction and disorder.
6. Teach or enhance competencies and coping skills.

7. Deepen social relationships and expand social network.

8. Explore psychological conflicts and   core pathogenic beliefs.

9. Facilitate disconfirming experiences for hopelessness and core pathogenic beliefs.

10. Create mechanisms for generalization and relapse prevention

B 4   CRISIS INTERVENTION FOR DISTRESSED PERSONS

1. Make psychological contact; establish relationship

    create opportunity to talk privately
    encourage talking
    listen
    be emphatic; communicate concern
    clarify and summarize facts and feelings

2. Explore dimensions of crisis/problem

    deal with immediate present
    focus on precipitating event
    facilitate awareness of person's reactions to stressor
    evaluate coping (e.g., lack of inappropriate coping)
    identify immediate needs, then eventual needs
    access suicide risk

3. Re-conceptualize meaning of crisis

    restate/reframe situation
    develop linkage between low self-esteem, current stressor
    ineffective coping, and hopelessness
    relate crisis to problem in current roles and relationships

4. Examine possible solutions

    what solutions already attempted
    brainstorm other alternatives to meeting needs
    emphasize and mobilize person's strengths and
    competencies

5. Assist in taking specific, concrete action

    problem-oriented and/or protection plan
    harness existing or previously effective coping strategies
    give advice
    involve significant others and utilize support network

6. Follow-up
    contract
    arrange procedure
    emphasize caring

B 5   MODIFIED HYPOGLYCEMIC DIET FOR PERSONS ON LITHIUM

The recommendations here are generally applicable for persons who experience weight gain on lithium. Specific recommendations for individuals should be obtained by a dietitian in cooperation with physician orders.

Avoid simple (refined) carbohydrates that involve high levels of sugar,

Increase complex carbohydrates such as breads, cereals and vegetables,

Increase high fiber foods such as fruits, vegetables and grains,

Decrease fat in your diet,

Eat a number of small meals and healthy snacks between meals.

NOTE:

This short list sounds like everything you have been hearing in the last years about what constitutes a healthy diet to decrease the risk of heart disease and cancer. Consequently, the person on lithium simply needs to eat a generally healthy diet.

WORKS CITED

Adolescent stress and depression. (1986). Teens in distress. University of Minnesota: Minnesota Extension Service.

Ardrey, R. (1961). African genesis: A personal investigation into the animal origins and nature of man. New York: Dell Publishing Co., Inc.

Burns, D. D., M.D. (1980). Feeling Good: The new mood therapy. New York: Signet Books.

Campbell, J. (1990). Transformations of myth through time. New York: Harper & Row.

Campbell Joseph & Bill Moyer, (1988), The Power of Myth. New York: Doubleday Dell Publishing Group Inc.

Diagnostic and Statistical Manual of Mental Disorders, Fourth Edition (1994) Washington DC: American Psychiatric Association.

Fawcett, J.A., MD (1991). Understanding the new risk factors for suicide. Lifesavers: The Newsletter of the American Suicide Foundation, 3:3.

Fawcett, J.A., MD (1992). Short- and long-term predictors of suicide in depressed patients. Lifesavers: The Newsletter of the American Suicide Foundation.

Fieve, F.R., MD (1975). Moodswings. New York: Bantam Books.

Fishman, K.D. (1991, June). Therapy for children. The Atlantic Monthly, pp. 47-69.

Gawain, S. (1978). Creative Visualizations. New York: Bantam Books.

Gelman, D. (1987, May 4). Depression. Newsweek. pp. 48-57.

Gold, M.S. (1987). The Good News About Depression. New York: Bantam Books.

Goode, E. (1990, March 5). Beating depression. U.S. News & World Report, pp. 48-55.

Hoberman, H.M., Ph.D. (1989). Completed suicide in children and adolescents: A review. In B.D. Garfinkel (Ed.), Adolescent suicide: Recognition, treatment, and prevention. New York: Haworth.

Jamison, K. (1994) Suicide and Manic-Depressive Illness, Lifesavers: The Newsletter of the American Suicide Foundation. 6:3

Klerman, G., Weissman, M., Rounsaville, B., & Chevron, E. (1984). Interpersonal psychotherapy of depression. New York: Basic Books, Inc.

McKay, M. & Fanning, P. (1987). Self esteem. Oakland, California: New Harbinger Publications.

McKnew, D.H., Cytryn, L., & Yahraes, H. (1983). Why isn't Johnny crying? Coping with depression in children. New York: Norton & Company.

Papolos, Demitri, MD & Papolos, Janice. (1997) Overcoming Depression. New York: HarperCollins.

Physicians' Desk Reference (1993) Montvale, N.J.: Medical Economics Company Inc.

Popper, C., MD (1989). Diagnosing bipolar vs. ADHD, American Academy of Child and Adolescent Psychiatry News. Washington DC

Restak, Richard, MD (1995) Brainscapes: An Introduction to What Neuroscience Has Learned about the Structure, Function, and Abilities of the Brain. New York: Hyperion.

Roy, A., (1992). Schizophrenia and suicide. Lifesavers: The Newsletter of the American Suicide Foundation.4:1

Sargent, M. (1989 a). Depressive illnesses: Treatment brings new hope. U.S. Department of Health and Human Services. National Institute of Mental Health.

Sheehan, D.V. (1983). The Anxiety disease. New York: Bantam Books.

Stevens, A. (1989). The Roots of War: A Jungian Perspective. New York: Paragon House.

Supporting young people following a suicide. (1986) Teens in Distress. University of Minnesota: Minnesota Extension Service.

Understanding the new risk factors for suicide. (1991, Summer). Lifesavers: The Newsletter of the American Suicide Foundation.

Useful information on suicide. (1986). U.S. Department of Health and Human Services. National Institute of Mental Health.

Weissman, M., Ph.D. (1991). Panic and suicidal behavior. Lifesavers: The Newsletter of the American Suicide Foundation.

FURTHER REFERENCES

Beck, Rush, Shaw and Emery, Cognitive Therapy of Depression (1979) Guilford Press, New York.

Burns, David D., MD (1993) Ten Days to Self-Esteem New York: Quill William Morrow.

Gorman, J.M., MD (1990) The Essential Guide to Psychiatric Drugs. New York: St. Martin's Press.

Hewett, J.H. (1980). After suicide. Philadelphia, Pennsylvania: The Westminster Press.

Kubler-Ross, Elisabeth. (1975). Death, the final growth stage. Prentice-Hall, Inc., Englewood Cliff, NJ

Larson, D.E., MD (Ed.). (1990). Mayo Clinic family health book. New York: William Morrow and Company, Inc.

Papolos, Demitri, MD and Papolos, Janice (1999) The Bipolar Child: The Definitive and Reassuriing Guide to Of Childhood's Most Misunderstood Disorder. New York: Broadway Books

Dowling, John, MD Creating Mind: How the Brain Works. (1998) New York: W. W. Norton & Company

Sargent, M. (1990). Helping the depressed person get treatment. U.S. Department of Health and Human Services. National Institute of Mental Health.

Sarnoff Schiff, H. (1977). The bereaved parent. NY: Penguin Books.

Veninga, R.L. (1985). A gift of hope: How we survive our tragedies. New York: Ballantine Books.

Wrobleski, A. (1991). Suicide survivors: A guide for those left behind. Minneapolis, Minnesota: Afterwords Publishing.

Youth Suicide Prevention Programs: A Resource Guide, National Center for Injury Prevention and Control, Centers for Disease Control, Mailstop F-36, 4770 Buford Highway NE, Atlanta, GA 30341

Helpful Organizations

Child and Adolescent Bipolar Foundation

Mission

CABF is a national, parent-led organization (not-for-profit status pending) with a professional advisory board of leading experts on early-onset bipolar disorders. Its mission is to educate families, professionals, and the public about bipolar disorders in children and adolescents. It supports families to maximize the well-being of the child while minimizing the adverse impact of bipolar disorders on the child and family. They advocate for increased services to families, and increased research on the nature, causes, and treatment of bipolar disorders in children and adolescents.

The Child and Adolescent Bipolar Foundation, 1187 Wilmette Ave., P.M.B. #331, Wilmette, IL 60091. Email : cabf.bpso.org , Web Site: www.cabf.org .

International Society for Bipolar Disorders

Mission

At this time no official mission statement is published. The unofficial mission stated at the Third International Conference on Bipolar Disorders is the

- Promotion of awareness of bipolar disorders in society at large;
- Promotion of awareness and education about this condition among mental health professionals;
- Fostering research on all aspects of bipolar disorder
- Continuation and promotion of international collaboration

Initial activities involve the publishing of a quarterly newsletter and the utilization of the new journal, Bipolar Disorders -- An International Journal of Psychiatry and Neurosciences.

Membership

Fee is $35 for members, $20 for trainees. A more permanent address may be available in the future, but initially it is: **International Society of Bipolar Disorders, c/o Samuel Gershon, MD, President-Elect, Department of Psychiatry, UPMC Health System, Western Psychiatric Institute & Clinic, 3811 O'Hara Street, Pittsburgh, PA 15213. For Further information phone: 412-383-3102**

Benline Press

Mission

Its focus is to publish books that will support families touched by depression and to address the importance of reducing unnecessary suffering of youngsters and young adults through initial screening. The message of using self-reporting scales twice a year in all schools starting at 4th grade is explained in print material and through lecture/workshops. For more information contact 1-**800-296-7163** or **Fax 1-218-525-9200** or visit www.benline.com.

NAMI

Mission

The mission of the National Alliance is to provide

- support groups across the country for seriously mentally ill individuals and their family members;
- information about treatment and services for seriously mentally ill individuals;
- advocacy on their behalf for needed treatment and services;
- public education about serious mental illnesses;
- campaigns to reduce the stigma that still surrounds serious mental illness; and
- campaigns to support brain research and research in psychiatric medication.

Membership
Individuals may join the National Alliance either by joining and AMI affiliate in their community or by joining NAMI directly. Contribute to NAMI are welcome.   NAMI's **800-950-NAMI** provides callers with information about the affiliates in their local area. **National Alliance for the Mentally Ill, 200 N. Glebe Road, Suite 1015, Arlington, VA   22203, Phone 703-524-7600, FAX 703-524-9094**

National DMDA

Mission
The mission of the National Depressive and Manic-Depressive Associations is to educate patients, families, mental health professionals, physicians, and the general public concerning the nature and management of depression and manic depression as treatable medical disorders; to foster self-help for patients and families, and to advocate for better access to care, more research, and the elimination of discrimination and stigma associated with these illnesses. They achieve these goals through the development and support   of self-help groups across the country.   Our membership includes people who have experienced depression and bipolar disorder, and their family members and friends.

Membership
The National DMDA is a not-for-profit organization directed by patients and their families. For a list of self-help groups in your area or membership information, contact National DMDA at **1-800-826-3632.. National Depressive and Manic-Depressive Association, 730 North Franklin Street, Suite 501, Chicago, IL 60610, Phone 312-642-0049, FAX   312-642-7243**

AFSP

Mission
The purpose of the American Foundation for Suicide Prevention AFSP is to advance knowledge about suicide and the ability to prevent it through the following activities:

- Encouraging the submission of outstanding research grant proposals, and funding the most promising of these projects in order to advance understanding of suicide;
- Serving as an informational and educational center with regard to suicide, in particular, assisting in the training of professionals in the treatment of suicidal individuals;
- Educating the public to the magnitude of the suicide problem and to the need for research, prevention, and treatment efforts with regard to suicide;
- Evaluating and helping to develop, and financially support programs that identify and treat the suicidal individual; and
- Supporting research, education, and programs directed to the problems of survivors of suicide.

Membership

Members of AFSP join by either becoming a member at $25, friend at $50, or contributor at $100. Each person who joins receives the <u>Lifesavers</u> quarterly newsletter which contains articles describing the newest research findings.
American Foundation For Suicide Prevention, 120 Wall Street, 22nd Floor, New York, NY 10005, Phone 212-363-3500, FAX 212-363-6237.

SPAN

Mission

The Suicide Prevention Advocacy Network exists to petition Congress to develop a proven, effective prevention program. It is a national, community-based, non-profit organization of survivors of suicide. Annually, people are asked to:
1. sign advocacy letters addressed to Congress and Governors
2. conduct suicide awareness programs to diminish shame
Span invites existing suicide prevention agencies to:
1. join the advocacy effort
2. freely share information on their initiatives

Membership

There are no dues-paying SPAN members; everyone who believes in the prevention of suicide is in fact a member. To make a working or financial contribution, or to find out about SPAN, readers can write to the address below, or call **1- 888-649-1366. SPAN, 5034 Odin's Way, Marietta, GA 30068, 770-998-8819 FAX 770-642-1419**

SA\VE

Mission In Action

SA\VE's programs for suicide prevention outreach at colleges, professional organizations, hospitals, mental health seminars, and all related conferences and workshops. SA\VE has a web site on the Internet which offers information to the general public. I distributes information through its office phone number, and at various public events. Outreach efforts include grief support groups, early response teams, and packets of information for first line responders. Public awareness campaigns have become the signature of SA\VE. The message, **"The #1 cause of suicide is untreated depression,"** is placed on billboards in various cities throughout the nation. TV and radio all have been used to help educate people. SA\VE also publishes a newsletter.

Membership

Annual membership is $35. Money offered as individual donations, or contributions in memory or in honor of a loved one are welcome. Members are encouraged to become volunteers. **SA\VE, P.O. Box 24507, Minneapolis, MN 55424-0507, Phone 612- 946-7998**

NOTE: Refer to page 219 for the *web addresses* of these and other helpful resources.

ABOUT THE AUTHOR

Trudy Carlson never intended to write this book. One year before the death of her son she was inspired to write a manuscript dealing with her life-long interest: the psychological interpretation of famous stories. Ben's death changed everything. She temporarily put the first book aside to begin writing the story of his life. She needed to record everything about the problems she observed during the various stages of his life, all the things she did to help him and the attempt to obtain treatment for his condition. The effect his life and death had on her became the focus of her writing.

As she worked she discovered she had three separate topics. The first became this book, The Suicide of My Son: A Story of Childhood Depression which has now been revised and expanded into this book, The Life of a Bipolar Child.

Learning Disabilities: How to Recognize & Manage Learning & Behavioral Problems in Children contrasts Ben's difficulty with ADHD with her own personal struggle with a mild case of dyslexia. The contrast between her success in overcoming her disability is explained in terms of the differences in the nature of the two learning problems. Generic no cost/low cost programs helpful for a wide range of difficulties faced by elementary aged youngsters today are described.

Tragedy, Finding a Hidden Meaning: How to Transform the Tragedies in Your Life into Personal Growth, explores the growth that can emerge from loss. It uses the wisdom found in enduring stories to demonstrate a way to discover a personal meaning in an otherwise seemingly meaningless tragedy. Carl Jung wrote, "Meaning makes most things endurable, perhaps everything." This book demonstrates how Ms. Carlson discovered meaning in her son's life and his death and is helpful to anyone experiencing a loss of any kind.

Suicide Survivors Handbook: A Guide for the Bereaved and Those Who Wish to Help Them, deals with the three major issues confronting the survivor: the question "why," anger over the death, and guilt. It describes the stages of grief and gives helpful suggestions for recovery. There are chapters on: "How do you deal with others?," "What about holidays?," and "What effect can the death have on you?"

ORDER FORM

Telephone orders: Call Toll Free: 1-800-296-7163

Postal Orders: Benline Press, 118 N. 60th Ave. E.
Duluth, MN   55804

Please send the following books. I understand that I may return any books for a full refund -- for any reason, no questions asked.

Suicide Survivor's Handbook: A Guide to the Bereaved and
Those Who Wish to Help Them—Expanded Edition
$15.95   _____

Tragedy, Finding a Hidden Meaning: How to Transform
the Tragedies in Your Life into Personal Growth $14.95   _____

Learning Disabilities: How to Recognize and Manage,
Learning and Behavioral Problems in Children $14.95   _____

Sales Tax: Please add 7.5% for books shipped to Minnesota addresses

Shipping: Book Rate: $2.00 for the first book and 75 cents for
each additional book (Surface shipping may take three
to four weeks)   Airmail: $3.50 per book
Total   _____